Home Cooking
with
Military Families

Home Cooking
with
Military Families

*Easy-to-prepare recipes
from U.S. service families around the
world*

Mary Jane Ryan
Executive Editor, FAMILY magazine

Stackpole Books

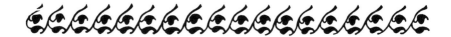

Published by
STACKPOLE BOOKS
Cameron and Kelker Streets
P.O. Box 1831
Harrisburg, PA 17105

10   9   8   7   6   5   4   3   2   1

Printed in the United States of America

Library of Congress Cataloging-in-Publication Data

Ryan, Mary Jane.
   Home cooking with military families.

   1. Cookery.   2. Military dependents.   I. Title.
TX715.R988   1987   641.5   86-23185
ISBN 0-8117-2106-X

Contents

Contents

Contents

Contents

Contents

Acknowledgments

I wish to thank the following people for their help in testing the recipes in this book: Joan Edwards, Will and Damian Glennon, Janice Kosel, Penny Layman, and Gloria and Vincent Ryan. Their aid was invaluable. In addition, I received much needed editorial assistance from Jean Vaine and Rick Weiss. Also worthy of thanks are Edward Koch and Joseph Mugnai, publishers of FAMILY magazine, who enabled me to put this cookbook together.

Finally, I would like to thank the hundreds of military families who submitted their recipes, those contained here as well as the ones we were unable to include. Without their participation, this cookbook literally would not exist.

Introduction

I had been toying with the idea of collecting the culinary efforts of military families for some time before the possibility of putting together this cookbook fell into my lap. As the executive editor of FAMILY, the magazine for military wives, for the past five years, I am well aware of the great interest military families have in cooking. FAMILY runs about 25 recipes in each issue, yet each time we do a readers' survey the number one request is for more recipes. Because of their mobile lifestyle, military families are exposed to cooking from around the world. I was certain that international exposure combined with budget constraints and the unavailability of certain foods on some bases would force military families to be very resourceful in their cooking. So when I received a letter from Stackpole Books saying they were interested in doing a collection of military family recipes, I jumped at the chance.

The result is this volume. The 200 recipes included here were culled from over 1,000 I received after posting announcements at base wives' clubs and in FAMILY magazine. Each one has been tested and, in some cases, modified. As a whole, they reflect the international exposure military families receive while keeping their roots firmly planted in the U.S.A. You will find that they are easy to prepare and will, I hope, add favorably to your mealtime repertoire.

The New Carleton House is the oldest building at Fort Huachuca, Arizona. Completed in 1880, it was the first hospital at the fort. *Drawing by Louis K. Smith, courtesy of Fort Huachuca.*

Appetizers

Bacon-Stuffed Mushrooms
Debbie Howard, Dyess AFB, Texas

     2 *pounds large fresh mushrooms*
     1 *stick butter or margarine*
     1 *medium onion, diced*
 8–10 *slices bacon, fried crisp and then crumbled*
     8 *crackers, crumbled*
   ⅛ *teaspoon dried thyme*
   ¼ *teaspoon fresh parsley, minced*
       pepper to taste
     2 *tablespoons grated Parmesan cheese (approximately)*

Wipe each mushroom clean and remove stem. Dice the stems.

In a medium skillet, melt the butter or margarine, then add mushroom stems and onion. Sauté over medium-high heat until onion is tender. Remove from heat.

Add the bacon, cracker crumbs, and spices. Stuff mixture into mushroom tops. Sprinkle each mushroom with Parmesan cheese.

Place on ungreased cookie sheet and bake in a preheated oven at 350°F for 10 minutes or until cheese is melted. Serves 6.

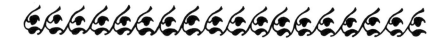

Corpus Christi Cheese Roll

Carol Barclay, Portland, Texas

    3 ounces cream cheese, softened
    ¼ cup sour cream
    3 tablespoons picante sauce or salsa
    ½ cup grated sharp cheddar cheese
    2 teaspoons chopped ripe olives
    1 tablespoon chopped green onion
    2 teaspoons chopped pimiento
    5 large flour tortillas

In a large bowl, beat the cream cheese to a creamy consistency. Blend the rest of the ingredients, except the tortillas, into the cheese.

Spread an even amount on each tortilla and roll up. Place on a plate seam side down and cover. Refrigerate overnight.

Slice on the diagonal into 1-inch slices. Serve with additional picante sauce or salsa. Makes 4 dozen.

Crab Cakes

Cassie Kolodgie, Nanticoke, Pennsylvania

    2 eggs, beaten
    2 tablespoons mayonnaise
  2-3 tablespoons flour
    1 tablespoon Dijon-style mustard
    1 tablespoon chopped fresh parsley
    1 tablespoon Worcestershire sauce
    1 1-pound can backfin crabmeat, shell removed
    ¼ cup cracker crumbs (approximately)
    ¼ cup vegetable oil (approximately)

Combine eggs, mayonnaise, 2 tablespoons flour, mustard, parsley, and Worchestershire sauce in a small bowl.

Shred the crabmeat into a large bowl. Pour the egg-spice mixture over the crab and work in gently. Add more flour if necessary to make mixture stick together.

Shape into hamburger-size patties and roll in cracker crumbs.

In a large skillet, heat the oil and add the crab cakes. Fry about 15 minutes or until browned on both sides. Serves 3.

Eggplant Puffs

Mrs. Dottie Rice, Virginia Beach, Virginia

1 *medium eggplant, peeled and cut into 2-inch cubes*
¾ *cup grated sharp cheddar cheese*
1 *egg, beaten*
¾ *cup bread crumbs*
¾ *teaspoon ground cumin*
¾ *teaspoon garlic powder*
2 *teaspoons lemon juice*
¼ *cup grated Parmesan cheese (optional)*
2 *tablespoons chopped fresh parsley (optional)*
½ *cup all-purpose flour (approximately)*
½ *cup vegetable oil (approximately)*

Boil eggplant in scant amount of water in a medium saucepan for about 10 minutes or until tender. Drain well and mash. Add cheddar cheese, egg, bread crumbs, and seasonings. Add Parmesan cheese and parsley if desired. Mix well.

Cover and refrigerate for at least 1 hour. Form mixture into 2-inch balls. Roll in flour.

Heat the oil in a wok or deep skillet to 325°F. Drop eggplant balls into the oil, 10 at a time, and fry until golden brown, about 3–5 minutes. Place on a paper-towel-lined plate to absorb excess grease. Serve immediately. Makes about 50.

Gail's Chili-Sauced Meatballs

Gail Guild, Vance AFB, Oklahoma

These meatballs can be kept warm and easily transported in a crock-pot.

> 2 *pounds ground beef*
> 2 *eggs*
> ⅓ *cup chopped fresh parsley*
> ⅓ *cup ketchup*
> ¼ *cup finely chopped onion*
> ¾ *cup bread crumbs*
> 1 *1-pound can jellied cranberry sauce*
> 1 *12-ounce bottle chili sauce*
> 2 *tablespoons brown sugar*
> 1 *tablespoon lemon juice*

In a large bowl, combine first 6 ingredients. Mix well with a fork. Shape mixture into 1-inch balls. Place in a 7 x 13 x 2-inch pan and set aside.

Combine remaining ingredients in a medium saucepan. Cook on medium-high heat, stirring often, until sauce is smooth. Pour over meatballs.

Bake, uncovered, in a preheated oven at 350°F for 30–40 minutes, stirring occasionally. Serves 12.

Mexican Ceviche

Evangelina Navarro, MacDill AFB, Florida

2 *pounds boneless white fish, such as sea bass or snapper*
8 *lemons*
½ *cup olive oil*
6 *tomatoes, chopped*
2 *green peppers, finely chopped*
2 *medium onions, sliced into rings*
2 *teaspoons salt*
1 *tablespoon dried oregano*
1 *teaspoon pepper*

Chop fish into bite-size pieces and place in a large glass bowl.

Squeeze lemons onto the fish, getting out as much of the juice as possible. Discard peels and pulp. Mix fish and lemon juice well. Cover and refrigerate at least 24 hours.

The next day, combine remaining ingredients in a small bowl. Add to fish mixture and mix well. Serves 6.

Mona's Party Paté

Mona L. Elliott, Fort Benjamin Harrison, Indiana

This paté is a prize-winner!

    1 *pound liverwurst sausage*
    ¼ *cup mayonnaise*
    1 *teaspoon Worcestershire sauce*
    8 *drops Tabasco sauce*
    ¼ *teaspoon garlic powder*
    2 *tablespoons horseradish*
    2 *8-ounce packages softened cream cheese, divided*
    ¾ *cup finely chopped onion*
    ¼ *cup finely chopped dill pickle*
    2 *tablespoons chopped fresh parsley (approximately)*

Mash liverwurst with a fork in a large bowl. Add mayonnaise, Worchestershire sauce, Tabasco, garlic powder, horseradish, 1 package cream cheese, onion, and pickle. Blend with an electric mixer on low until smooth. Cover and chill overnight.

Remove from refrigerator and shape into a ball. Frost with remaining package of cream cheese. Sprinkle with parsley. Serve with crackers. Serves 10.

Sausage Ryes
Mrs. Dolores A. Diehl, Minot AFB, North Dakota

1 *pound bulk pork*
sausage
1 *pound Velveeta cheese*
¼ *teaspoon garlic salt*
¼ *teaspoon onion salt*
¼ *teaspoon oregano*
2 *tablespoons ketchup*
1 *16-ounce loaf party rye*

In a medium skillet, brown sausage slowly. Drain and return to skillet.

With heat on low, add cheese, spices, and ketchup. Stir constantly until cheese melts. Remove from heat.

Spread on party rye, using about 1 tablespoon per slice of bread.

Place on ungreased cookie sheet and bake in a preheated oven at 350°F for 10 minutes or until bubbly. Serves 12.

Simple Tofu Appetizer
Gail Ann Kenna, Maxwell AFB, Alabama

This appetizer is in line with the cardiovascular health advice given to military families at the Air War College in Montgomery, Alabama. It offers a minimum of calories and fat.

> 1 *16-ounce package firm tofu*
> ½ *cup soy sauce*
> 2 *tablespoons granulated sugar*
> 2 *tablespoons dry sherry*
> ¼ *teaspoon ground ginger*
> 2 *cloves garlic, minced*
> ½ *cup all-purpose flour*
> ¼ *cup sesame seeds*
> 1 *tablespoon vegetable oil (approximately)*
> 2 *tablespoons chopped green onion (optional)*

Rinse the tofu, drain in a colander, and cut into 1-inch cubes. Set aside.

Make the marinade by combining soy sauce, sugar, sherry, ginger, and garlic in a medium bowl. Marinate tofu for 5–10 minutes, turning the cubes to coat well.

Combine flour and sesame seeds in a small bowl. Using a slotted spoon, lift each tofu cube from the marinade and dip in flour-sesame seed mixture. Be sure to coat all sides.

Heat the oil in a large frying pan or wok over medium heat. Add about one-third of the tofu at a time and cook until lightly browned on all sides. Add more oil if needed.

Place browned tofu on paper towels. Serve warm, with chopped green onions if desired. Pass the marinade as a dipping sauce. Serves 10.

Spinach Balls

Gail Guild, Vance AFB, Oklahoma

These freeze well before or after baking.

> 2 *10-ounce packages chopped spinach*
> 2 *cups shredded stuffing*
> 6 *eggs, beaten*
> 2 *onions, minced*
> ½ *cup grated Parmesan cheese*
> ¾ *cup melted butter or margarine*
> 1 *teaspoon pepper*
> 1 *teaspoon thyme*
> 1½ *teaspoons garlic powder*

Cook spinach according to package directions and drain very well. Combine with remaining ingredients in a large bowl. Mix well. Shape into 2-inch balls.

Place on a greased cookie sheet and bake in a preheated oven at 350°F for 20 minutes or until balls are lightly browned. Serves 15.

Texas Egg Rolls
Carol Barclay, Portland, Texas

These eggrolls can be frozen, uncooked, on cookie sheets and placed in plastic bags. To use, defrost and fry them.

> 2 *pounds ground beef*
> 2 *medium onions, finely chopped*
> 1 *clove garlic, crushed*
> 1½ *teaspoon salt*
> ½ *teaspoon dried oregano*
> 1 *teaspoon ground cumin*
> 4 *cups shredded cheddar cheese*
> 24 *whole canned green chilies*
> 24 *egg roll wrappers*
> 1 *egg, beaten*
> ¼ *cup water*
> 1 *quart vegetable oil (approximately)*

Brown beef in a large skillet over medium heat. Drain off excess grease. Add onion, garlic, and seasonings. Stir and cook until onion is tender, about 10 minutes.

Remove from heat. Add cheese and blend well. Set aside.

Remove seeds from chilies, spread open and pat dry with a paper towel. Fill each chili with 2 tablespoons meat mixture. Roll up like a jelly roll.

In a small bowl, combine egg and water. Set aside.

Place each filled chili diagonally on an egg roll wrapper. Wrap as follows: Lift lower triangle flap over chilie and tuck the point under. Bring left and right corners toward the center and roll, sealing all edges with egg mixture.

Heat oil to 325°F in a wok or deep skillet. Deep-fry egg rolls 3–4 at a time until golden brown.

Place on a paper-towel lined plate to absorb excess grease. Serve immediately with picante sauce or salsa, if desired. Makes 24 egg rolls.

Texas Riviera Seafood Dip
Carol Barclay, Portland, Texas

1 8-ounce package cream cheese, softened
1 tablespoon mayonnaise
¼ teaspoon Worcestershire sauce
  juice of 1 lemon
½ teaspoon seasoned salt
½ teaspoon lemon pepper
1 12-ounce jar cocktail sauce
1 6-ounce can crabmeat, drained and flaked
4 ounces Monterey Jack cheese, shredded
2 ounces mozzarella cheese, shredded
6 green onions, chopped
½ green pepper, chopped
½ cup chopped ripe olives
1 tomato, chopped

In a medium bowl, mix cream cheese till smooth. Add mayonnaise, Worcestershire sauce, lemon juice, salt, and pepper. Mix well. Spread this mixture in the bottom of a 9 x 13-inch dish or glass pizza plate.

Layer remaining ingredients on top of the cream cheese as follows: cocktail sauce, crab, Jack cheese, mozzarella cheese, green onions, green pepper, olives, and tomatoes.

Serve at room temperature with melba toast or crackers. Serves 15.

Vickie's Dill Dip
Vickie L. Brown, San Jose, California

1 *cup sour cream*
1 *cup mayonnaise*
2 *teaspoons dried dill weed*
2 *teaspoons dried parsley flakes*
2 *teaspoons Lowry's Seasoned Salt*

In a medium bowl, combine all ingredients. Stir well. Cover and refrigerate for at least 1 hour. Serve with raw vegetables. Will keep in refrigerator for up to 1 week. Serves 10.

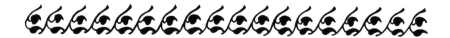

Wonton Tommy

Lt. T. J. Henning, Whiting Field, Milton, Florida

1½ pounds ground beef
10 ounces frozen popcorn shrimp, thawed
½ pound fresh mushrooms, diced
1 5¼-ounce can pineapple chunks, drained and diced
1 stalk celery, diced
½ medium onion, diced
¼ teaspoon M.S.G.
1 teaspoon chopped fresh parsley
½ cup firmly packed brown sugar
⅓ cup all-purpose flour
⅓ cup water
1 1-pound package wonton wrappers
4–5 cups vegetable oil

Mix first 9 ingredients in a large bowl. Cover and refrigerate for 1 hour.

Combine the flour and water in a small bowl to make a paste.

Place 1 heaping tablespoon of beef and shrimp mixture in the center of a wonton wrapper. Fold the 4 corners into the center, securing with a dab of flour paste. Repeat with each wrapper.

Heat the oil to 325°F in deep fat fryer. Keeping oil very hot, drop the wontons in, 6 or 7 at a time, and fry until golden brown, about 3–5 minutes.

Place on a paper-towel-lined plate to absorb grease. Serve immediately with sweet and sour sauce or hot mustard. Serves 8.

Soups

Broccoli-Cheese Noodle Soup

Susan D. Smith, Las Vegas, Nevada

    2 tablespoons vegetable oil
    ¾ cup chopped onion
    6 cups water
    6 chicken bouillon cubes
    8 ounces fine egg noodles, uncooked
    1 teaspoon salt
    2 10-ounce packages frozen chopped broccoli, unthawed
    ¼ teaspoon garlic powder
    6 cups milk
    1 pound American cheese, cubed
      dash pepper

Heat oil in large kettle or Dutch oven. Add onion and cook over medium heat for 3 minutes or until onion is tender.

Add water and bouillon cubes. Bring to a boil, stirring occasionally, until cubes are dissolved. Gradually add noodles and salt so that mixture continues to boil. Cook, uncovered, for 3 minutes, stirring occasionally.

Stir in broccoli and garlic powder. Cook 4 minutes, stirring occasionally.

Add milk, cheese and pepper. Stir constantly over low heat until cheese melts. Serves 10.

Chicken Bisque Soup
Margaret Quinn Potter, USMA, West Point, New York

2   tablespoons butter
2   tablespoons flour
3   cups chicken stock, homemade or canned
1   cup chopped cooked chicken
½   cup minced celery
1   cup whipping cream
    salt to taste
    paprika to taste
    dash mace

Melt the butter in a medium saucepan. Whisk in the flour until a smooth paste is formed. Add the chicken stock and stir until liquid thickens and comes to a boil.

Add chicken and celery. Cook on low heat at least 30 minutes.

Scald cream in a small saucepan and add to soup mixture. Season with salt, paprika, and mace. Serves 5.

Cream of Leek Soup
Mary McCool, Tinker AFB, Oklahoma

  1 *pound leeks*
  2 *tablespoons butter or margarine*
  3 *tablespoons flour*
  1 *teaspoon chicken broth*
    dash nutmeg
  1 *cup water*
2½ *cups milk*
  ½ *cup shredded cheddar or Swiss cheese*
    salt and pepper to taste

Wash leeks very thoroughly. Cut off roots. Cut each leek into small circles, using all of the white part and about ½ inch of the green.

Boil leeks in water in a small saucepan until tender. Drain.

In a medium saucepan, melt butter or margarine and stir in flour, broth, and nutmeg. Add water and milk. Cook and stir over low heat until thickened and bubbly, about 5 minutes.

Add leeks and cheese. Cook gently until cheese has melted and soup is hot. Do not boil. Season with salt and pepper. Serves 2.

Cream of Turkey Soup

Jeanie Reed, Camp Lejeune, North Carolina

1 *pound turkey wings*
2 *quarts water*
1 *teaspoon salt*
1 *medium onion, sliced*
2 *stalks celery with leaves, chopped*
1 *bay leaf*
2 *tablespoons butter or margarine*
¼ *cup all-purpose flour*
3 *tablespoons lemon juice*
1 *10-ounce package frozen carrots*
1 *10-ounce package frozen peas*
¼ *cup heavy cream*

Rinse turkey wings and put in a Dutch oven with water, salt, onion, celery, and bay leaf. Bring to a boil. Cover and simmer 1½ hours.

Strain broth and reserve vegetables and liquid. Skin and bone turkey wings. Set turkey meat aside.

Melt butter or margarine in Dutch oven. Stir in flour. Cook 3 minutes. Slowly whisk in reserved broth. Add lemon juice and carrots. Cover and simmer 7 minutes.

Add peas, reserved turkey, and vegetables. Simmer 3 minutes. Pour in cream. Heat thoroughly on low but do not allow to boil. Serves 4.

Deb's Clam Chowder

Deborah A. Howard, Dyess AFB, Texas

3 6½-ounce cans clams, with juice
1½ sticks butter or margarine
1 medium onion, chopped
1 cup water
4 cups diced potatoes
1 carrot, grated
2 tablespoons dried parsley
¼ teaspoon red pepper
1 12-ounce can evaporated milk
4 cups milk, divided
½ cup plus 1 tablespoon all-purpose flour

Drain clams, reserving juice.

Melt the butter or margarine in a Dutch oven. Add drained clams and onion. Sauté on medium-high heat for about 10 minutes, or until onion is tender.

Add the reserved clam juice, water, potatoes, carrot, parsley, and red pepper. Cover and cook on medium-high heat until potatoes are tender, about 15 minutes.

Turn the heat to low and add the evaporated milk and 3 cups milk. Heat gently to simmering point.

Combine the remaining 1 cup milk and the flour in a small bowl. Stir well. Pour slowly through a strainer into chowder, stirring constantly until soup thickens. Do not allow to boil. Serve when heated thoroughly. Serves 6.

Green Chili Cheese Soup
Mrs. Toni Woods, Schofield Barracks, Hawaii

1 quart water
3 medium potatoes, cubed
½ cup chopped onion
2 tomatoes, diced
3 cloves garlic
1 3-ounce can chopped green chilies
1 cup milk
½ pound Monterey Jack cheese, cubed
    salt and pepper to taste

Bring water to boil in a large saucepan. Add potatoes, onion, tomatoes, garlic, and green chilies. Bring to a boil, cover and simmer 15 minutes.

Add milk and cook for 20 minutes over low heat, stirring occasionally. Turn off heat and add cheese. Let stand for 5 minutes or until cheese melts. Stir. Add salt and pepper. Serves 6.

Ham and Wild Rice Soup
Lynn Gardner, Davis-Monthan AFB, Arizona

This soup is great with some French bread and white wine.

> ¾ *cup raw wild rice*
> 1 *tablespoon vegetable oil*
> 1 *quart water*
> ½ *cup butter or margarine*
> 1 *large onion, diced*
> 1 *stalk celery, diced*
> 1 *carrot, diced*
> ½ *cup all-purpose flour*
> 3 *cups chicken broth*
> 1 *cup diced, cooked ham*
> 2 *cups half-and-half or milk*
> *salt and pepper to taste*
> ½ *teaspoon dried rosemary*
> ½ *teaspoon dried parsley (optional)*

Rinse and drain wild rice. In a Dutch oven, sauté in oil until lightly browned. Add the water, cover and cook over medium-high heat for 30 minutes.

Drain rice, reserving liquid. If necessary, add enough water to equal 1½ cups. Set aside.

Remove rice and set aside.

Melt the butter in the Dutch oven. Over medium-high heat, sauté onion, celery, and carrot until onion is tender, about 10 minutes. Reduce heat.

Blend in flour and cook, stirring, on low for about 5 minutes. Do not allow to brown. Whisk in chicken broth and reserved rice water. Bring to a boil, stirring constantly. Once boiling, stir for 1 minute.

Add the rice, ham, half-and-half or milk, and seasonings. Heat gently uncovered for about 20 minutes. Do not allow to boil. Serves 6.

Hearty Bean Soup

Olwen Ann Stephens, Aurora, Colorado

3 slices uncooked bacon, cut into 2-inch pieces
1 medium onion, sliced
1 large carrot, thinly sliced
1 large stalk celery, sliced
1 clove garlic, finely chopped
5 cups water, divided
2 cups uncooked lentils
1 cube chicken bouillon
2 tablespoons chopped fresh parsley
1 tablespoon salt
½ teaspoon pepper
½ teaspoon dried thyme
1 bay leaf
1 28-ounce can whole tomatoes, crushed

Fry bacon in Dutch oven until limp. Set bacon aside, reserving bacon drippings.

Add onion, carrot, celery, and garlic to bacon fat. Cook, stirring, over medium heat until celery is tender, about 10 minutes.

Stir in bacon, 4 cups of water, lentils, bouillon cube, parsley, salt pepper, thyme, and bay leaf. Bring to a boil, cover and reduce heat. Simmer until soup thickens, about 1 hour.

Add tomatoes and 1 cup water. Simmer, uncovered, for 15 minutes. Serves 8.

Italian Split Pea Soup

Mrs. Joni R. Terrio, Atwater, California

  1 1-pound bag split peas, washed and drained
  1 large onion, diced
  2 medium potatoes, diced
  2 medium carrots, diced
  1 4-ounce can garbanzo beans, drained
  2 stalks celery, diced
  1 teaspoon garlic salt
  ½ teaspoon dried tarragon
  ½ teaspoon dried basil
  ½ teaspoon dried oregano
  1 16-ounce can whole tomatoes, crushed
  ½ cup diced black olives
  2 medium zucchini, cut into ½-inch cubes

In a large Dutch oven, place the split peas and onion with enough water to cover. Bring to a boil, then cover and turn down heat. Simmer for 2 hours, adding more water if necessary.

After 2 hours, add remaining ingredients except olives and zucchini. Add more water if necessary. Bring to a boil, cover and simmer for 45 minutes on medium-low heat.

During the last 10 minutes, add the olives and zucchini. Serves 6.

Lentil Delight

Danielle Jones, Panama Canal Zone

2 tablespoons butter or margarine
1 stalk celery, finely chopped
1 onion, finely chopped
1 small green pepper, finely chopped
1 teaspoon dried basil
1 teaspoon dried thyme
1 teaspoon dried oregano
1 teaspoon dried tarragon
1 bay leaf
1 teaspoon garlic powder
5 cups water or vegetable broth
½ cup uncooked lentils
1 cup green beans, finely chopped
2 carrots, diced
1 cup frozen corn, thawed
½ cup frozen green peas, thawed
¼ cup tomato paste
⅓ cup tomato sauce
　 salt and pepper to taste

Melt butter in a large stewpot. Add the celery, onion, green pepper, basil, thyme, oregano, tarragon, and bay leaf. Sauté until tender. Add the garlic and sauté for 2 more minutes.

Add the water or broth. Bring to a boil. Add the lentils, green beans, carrots, corn, and peas. Bring to a boil, then lower heat. Cover and simmer for 1½ hours, stirring occasionally.

Add the tomato paste, tomato sauce, salt, and pepper. Cover and simmer another 15 minutes. Serves 4.

Pasta Fagioli

Fran Mugnai, Old Westbury, New York

This heartwarming "peasant soup," concocted to fill the stomachs of poor Italians, has become a staple among Italians and Italian Americans. Variations include using different shapes of macaroni and adding prosciutto or bacon.

> ¼ *cup olive oil*
> 2 *cloves garlic, crushed*
> 1 *16-ounce can tomato sauce*
> 1 *19-ounce can white kidney beans, undrained*
> ½ *teaspoon dried oregano*
>   *salt and pepper to taste*
> ½ *pound ditali macaroni, cooked according to*
>   *package directions*

Heat oil in a Dutch oven and cook garlic until golden brown. Add tomato sauce, beans, and spices. Simmer, covered for ½ hour.

Add cooked macaroni and simmer, covered, for 10–12 minutes more. Serves 4.

Pennsylvania Dutch Chicken Soup
Dee Aldrich, Chester, Virginia

1 *fryer (about 3 pounds), cut in pieces*
1 *large onion, coarsely chopped*
1 *stalk celery with leaves, chopped*
3 *chicken bouillon cubes*
  salt and pepper to taste
2 *quarts water*
5 *medium potatoes, diced*
2 *16-ounce cans shoe peg corn, drained*
½ *teaspoon chopped fresh parsley*
2 *hardboiled eggs, chopped (optional)*
  few drops cider vinegar (optional)

In a large pot with a tight-fitting lid, cook chicken, onion, celery, bouillon cubes, salt, pepper, and water on medium heat for about 1 hour or until chicken is tender.

Drain chicken, reserving broth. Discard skin and vegetables. Debone chicken and cut into bite-size pieces.

Return chicken and broth to pot. Add potatoes. Cook, uncovered, on medium heat until potatoes are tender, about 15 minutes.

Add corn and parsley. Cook over medium heat until corn is hot, about 5 minutes. Add chopped eggs and vinegar, if desired. Serves 6.

Sausage-Bean Chowder

Carol Bisbee, Little Creek NAB, North Carolina

½ pound mild sausage
1 pound raw kidney beans, soaked in water overnight and drained
1½ cups tomatoes
2 cups water
1 onion, chopped
1 bay leaf
½ teaspoon salt
1 teaspoon garlic powder
½ teaspoon pepper
½ cup diced potatoes
¼ cup diced green pepper

In a large stewpot, cook sausage until tender, about 15 minutes. Drain.

Return sausage to pot and add remaining ingredients. Bring to a boil, cover, and lower the heat. Simmer until beans are done, about 4 hours, stirring occasionally. Add water if needed. Serves 6.

Sharon's Chowder with a Twist

Sharon McAtee, Bolling AFB, Maryland

This dish is great for those evenings when you don't know how long an "exercise" will last.

2 *cups water*
2 *cups diced potatoes*
½ *cup diced carrots*
½ *cup diced celery*
¼ *cup diced onion*
1 *teaspoon salt*
¼ *teaspoon pepper*
½ *cup butter or margarine*
¼ *cup flour*
2 *cups milk*
½ *teaspoon dry mustard*
2 *cups grated cheddar cheese*
1 *cup diced, cooked ham*
¼–½ *cup croutons*

In a Dutch oven, combine the first 7 ingredients. Bring to a boil, cover and simmer until potatoes and carrots are tender, about 10–15 minutes.

Meanwhile, melt the butter in a medium-size saucepan. Add the flour, stir and let cook for 1 minute. Slowly whisk in milk and dry mustard, stirring constantly over low heat until thickened. Do not allow to boil.

Remove from heat and add cheese. Stir constantly until cheese melts. Add ham and cheese sauce to undrained vegetables in Dutch oven. Heat gently but do not allow to boil. Place in individual serving bowls and top with croutons. Serves 4.

Salads

Asparagus Soup Mousse
Mrs. Billie C. Spell, Littleton, North Carolina

1 *envelope unflavored gelatin*
½ *cup cold water*
1 *10¾-ounce can condensed cream of asparagus soup*
¾ *cup sour cream*
   hardboiled egg slices, cooked asparagus spears,
   tomato wedges (optional)

In a small saucepan, combine gelatin and water. Heat slowly to dissolve. Cool slightly. Add soup and mix well. Stir in sour cream.

Spoon into an 8 x 8 x 2-inch Pyrex dish or pan. Chill until firm, about 1 hour. Cut into serving portions, remove, and serve on leaf lettuce. Garnish with egg slices, asparagus spears, and tomato wedges if desired. Serves 4.

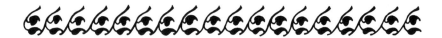

Borscht Salad

Beth Thompson, Savannah, Georgia

This salad goes well with heavy German dishes.

  1 *1-pound, 4-ounce can crushed pineapple, undrained*
  1 *6-ounce package raspberry gelatin*
1½ *cups boiling water*
  1 *1-pound can shoestring beets, undrained*
  3 *tablespoons vinegar*
1½ *tablespoons dried dill weed, divided*
  1 *cup chopped celery*
  ½ *cup sour cream (approximately)*

Drain pineapple, reserving syrup.

In a large mixing bowl, dissolve gelatin in boiling water. Stir in beets, beet liquid, vinegar, 1 tablespoon dill weed, and pineapple syrup. Chill until mixture begins to thicken, about 15–20 minutes.

Fold in celery and pineapple. Pour into 6-cup mold. Refrigerate until firm, at least 2 hours.

Unmold and serve with dollops of sour cream sprinkled with remaining dill weed. Serves 12.

Broccoli-Cauliflower Vinaigrette
Cynthia Lopreiato, Charleston, South Carolina

Salad
1 medium head cauliflower
1 pound fresh broccoli

Dressing
1 cup vinegar
1 cup vegetable oil
1 tablespoon granulated sugar
1 tablespoon M.S.G.
1 tablespoon dried dill
1 teaspoon salt
1 teaspoon pepper

Wash the cauliflower and broccoli and cut into bite-size pieces. In a large steamer, steam over boiling water for 5 minutes. Rinse in cold water. Drain thoroughly. Combine broccoli and cauliflower in a large, nonmetallic bowl.

In a screw-top jar, combine dressing ingredients. Cover and shake well to mix.

Pour dressing over broccoli and cauliflower. Toss thoroughly. Refrigerate several hours or overnight. Drain off dressing and serve. Serves 6.

Cabbage Cottage Salad

Joyce Lovette Fetters, Norfolk Naval Base, Virginia

½ small green cabbage
½ cup small-curd cottage cheese
⅓ cup mayonnaise
2 tablespoons chopped onion
¼ teaspoon celery seed
¼ teaspoon salt
   dash pepper

Shred cabbage and place in medium bowl. Add remaining ingredients and toss well. Serves 4.

Chinese Salad
Carol Wheeler, Hill AFB, Utah

Salad
- 1 *head lettuce, shredded*
- 4 *green onions, chopped*
- 2 *tablespoons slivered almonds, toasted*
- 2 *ounces wonton wrappers, cut into 2-inch strips and deep fried according to package directions*
- 1 *tablespoon sesame seeds, toasted*
- 4 *ounces Mei-fun noodles, deep fried according to package directions*

Dressing
- 3 *tablespoons granulated sugar*
- 2 *teaspoons salt*
- 1 *teaspoon M.S.G.*
- 1 *teaspoon pepper*
- ¼ *cup vegetable oil*
- 2 *tablespoons sesame oil*
- 6 *tablespoons Japanese rice vinegar*

Mix all salad ingredients in a large serving bowl.

To make dressing, combine all dressing ingredients in a small bowl or jar with a tight-fitting lid. Combine well and pour over salad. Put dressing on just before serving. Serves 8.

Curly Pasta Salad
Hazel Kerley, San Diego, California

Salad
- 1 12-ounce package curly pasta, cooked until just tender and drained according to package directions
- 1 cup chopped celery
- 1 cup chopped red onion
- ½ cup chopped green pepper
- ½ cup chopped sweet red pepper
- ¼ cup chopped fresh parsley
- 2 4-ounce jars pimiento strips, drained
- 1 6-ounce can sliced ripe olives, drained
- 1 6-ounce jar stuffed green olives, drained and sliced
- 1 8-ounce can water chestnuts, drained and sliced
- 2 6½-ounce jars marinated artichoke hearts, drained and chopped
- 1 10-ounce package frozen chopped broccoli, cooked according to package directions until just tender
- 1 10-ounce package frozen peas, thawed
- ¼ small head cauliflower, cut into flowerets and cooked until just tender

Dressing
- juice of 1 lemon
- ½ cup rice or tarragon vinegar
- 2 cloves garlic, chopped
- 2 tablespoons grated Parmesan cheese
- salt and pepper to taste
- 1 tablespoon dried basil
- 1 tablespoon dried oregano
- ¾ cup olive oil

In a large bowl, combine all salad ingredients. Toss gently but thoroughly.

Using a jar with a screw top, combine all dressing ingredients and shake well. Pour over salad and toss gently. Let sit 6–8 hours before serving so flavors can blend. Serves 12.

Easy Gourmet Cucumber Salad
Sylvia Radom, Miami, Florida

2 medium cucumbers
  salt
2 tablespoons mayonnaise
1 teaspoon Dijon-style mustard
¼ teaspoon garlic powder
1 tablespoon fresh dill or 1 teaspoon dried dill
  salt and pepper to taste

Peel cucumbers and slice paper-thin. Sprinkle with salt and place in a colander for 30 minutes. Wash off salt with cold water and squeeze excess water out of cucumbers with your hands.

In a medium bowl, combine remaining ingredients. Add cucumbers. Mix well and chill for at least 1 hour. Serves 4.

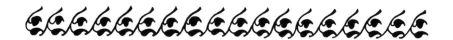

Fresh Broccoli Salad

Mrs. John (Marian) Ramey, Fort McPherson, Georgia

Salad
1 bunch broccoli, cut up
1 cup raisins
6 slices bacon, fried and crumbled
½ pound fresh mushrooms, sliced
½ cup chopped onion

Dressing
1 egg
½ cup granulated sugar
½ teaspoon dry mustard
2 teaspoons cornstarch
¼ cup white vinegar
¼ cup water
¼ teaspoon salt
2 tablespoons butter or margarine, softened
½ cup mayonnaise

In a large bowl, combine salad ingredients. Set aside.

Whisk together egg, sugar, mustard, and cornstarch in a small bowl.

In a medium saucepan, combine vinegar, water, and salt. Bring to a boil over medium heat. Whisk in egg mixture and cook, whisking constantly, for 1 minute or until mixture has thickened. Remove from heat and whisk in butter or margarine, then mayonnaise. Cover and refrigerate until chilled, about 1 hour.

Pour over salad when chilled thoroughly. Toss well and serve immediately. Serves 6.

Frozen Fruit Salad

Carol Barclay, Portland, Texas

1 14-ounce can condensed milk
⅓ cup lemon juice
2 10-ounce packages sliced frozen strawberries,
   thawed
1 15¼-ounce can crushed pineapple, undrained
2 bananas, mashed
1 13-ounce carton Cool Whip
1 cup chopped pecans

In a large bowl, combine all ingredients, using an electric mixer at low speed until evenly mixed.

Pour into paper or foil muffin wrappers that have been placed in muffin tins. Cover and freeze overnight. Serve frozen. Serves 8.

G&G Salad

Mrs. Vivian Joan Neal, Mayport NAS, Florida

> 1 cup green peas, fresh or frozen
> ½ cup cheddar cheese, shredded
> 2 tablespoons diced onion
> ½ tablespoon mustard
> 1 tablespoon mayonnaise
>   dash salt and pepper

If using frozen peas, cook according to package directions. If using fresh, steam them for 3 minutes and let cool.

In a medium serving dish, mix peas, cheese, and onion. Then add remaining ingredients and mix well. Serves 5.

Gazpacho Salad

Dixie L. Anderson, Mount Holly, New Jersey

5 *slices French or Italian bread*
1 *cucumber, unpeeled*
2 *large ripe tomatoes*
1 *large sweet Spanish or Bermuda onion*
1 *cup mayonnaise*
   salt and pepper to taste

Dry slices of bread on counter for 2 or 3 days until very hard. (If you have a gas oven with a pilot light, place bread in unlit oven for 4–6 hours.) Break bread into cubes.

Quarter and slice cucumber into ¼-inch pieces. Cut tomatoes into chunks. Slice onion into large crescents.

In a medium bowl, mix all ingredients with mayonnaise, salt, and pepper. Store in refrigerator overnight to allow all flavors to mingle. Serves 4.

Japanese Cucumber Salad
Evangelina Navarro, MacDill AFB, Florida

2 tablespoons white vinegar
1 tablespoon sesame oil
⅛ teaspoon dry mustard
¼ cup soy sauce
¼ teaspoon Tabasco sauce
2 medium cucumbers
1 tablespoon sesame seeds, toasted

In a small jar, combine vinegar, sesame oil, dry mustard, soy sauce, and Tabasco sauce. Cover and shake well.

Score cucumbers by running the tines of a fork down all sides of each cucumber. Thinly slice.

In a medium serving dish, combine cucumbers and dressing. Sprinkle with sesame seeds. Serves 4.

Layered Vegetable Salad

Mrs. James D. Smith II, Killeen, Texas

2 *cups cottage cheese*
2 *tablespoons mayonnaise*
1 *teaspoon salt*
½ *teaspoon white pepper*
1 *tablespoon grated onion*
1 *head Boston lettuce, chopped*
1 *16-ounce can sliced beets, drained*
1 *cucumber, thinly sliced*
1 *medium onion, thinly sliced into rings*
2 *large tomatoes, thinly sliced*
3 *tablespoons chopped fresh chives*

Mix cottage cheese with mayonnaise, salt, pepper, and grated onion in a small bowl. Set aside.

Line a large, straight-sided, glass salad bowl with lettuce. Coat with 3 tablespoons of cottage cheese mixture. Add beets, then cucumber, onion rings, and tomatoes, in that order. Cover with remaining cottage cheese mixture. Sprinkle with chives.

Cover tightly and refrigerate at least 4 hours before serving. Do not toss before serving. Serves 10.

Linguine Salad
Romona R. DeWolf, Fort Lee, Virginia

1 *pound linguine, cooked and drained according to package directions*
1 *8-ounce bottle Italian salad dressing*
½ *2.75-ounce bottle Schilling Salad Supreme seasoning**
1 *cucumber, peeled and sliced*
2 *medium tomatoes, sliced*
1 *medium onion, chopped*
2 *medium carrots, grated*
2 *celery stalks, chopped*

To the hot linguine, add salad dressing and seasoning. Mix well. Cover and refrigerate at least 1 hour. Just before serving, add rest of ingredients and toss well. Serves 6.

---

* A combination of dried spices and cheeses.

Mother-in-Law Cole Slaw
Jean Potter Klotzbach, Columbia, Maryland

Salad
1 *large head green cabbage, finely chopped*
1 *large onion, finely chopped*
⅞ *cup granulated sugar*

Dressing
2 *tablespoons granulated sugar*
¾ *teaspoon salt*
1 *teaspoon dry mustard*
1 *teaspoon celery seed*
¾ *cup vegetable oil*
1 *cup white vinegar*

Put cabbage and onion in a large pail. Pour sugar over top but do not stir. Set aside while making dressing.

Combine all dressing ingredients in a medium saucepan. Bring slowly to a rolling boil, stirring constantly. When mixture has come to full boil, remove from heat and pour over cabbage. Do not stir.

Cover pail and let sit in a cool place for 15–25 minutes. When mixture is cool, stir well.

Place in a 1-gallon glass jar with a tight-fitting lid. Place in refrigerator for at least 3 days. Stir before serving. Keeps up to a month in refrigerator. Serves 10.

Paper Cup Salad

Carol A. Bisbee, Little Creek NAB, Virginia

2 cups sour cream
2 tablespoons lemon juice
½ cup granulated sugar
1 8-ounce can crushed pineapple, drained
1 diced banana
¼ cup chopped nuts (optional)
1 1-pound can pitted cherries, drained

In a large mixing bowl, combine all ingredients and stir well. Pour mixture into muffin tins that have been lined with paper baking cups. Freeze 8–12 hours.

Remove from freezer approximately 30 minutes before serving. Serves 12.

Sauerkraut Salad

Mrs. Thomas A. (Shirley J.) Redden, Los Angeles, California

> 2 cups drained sauerkraut
> ½ cup chopped onion
> ½ cup chopped green pepper
> ½ cup chopped celery
> 1 1-pound can garbanzo beans, drained
> 1 4-ounce jar chopped pimientos
> 2 teaspoons celery seed
> 1½ teaspoons mustard seed
> 1 cup granulated sugar
> 1 tablespoon red wine vinegar

Combine all ingredients in a nonmetallic bowl. Stir well. Cover and refrigerate at least 10–12 hours before serving. Will keep in refrigerator for 5–7 days. Serves 6.

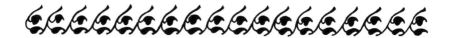

Sweet and Simple Salad

Iva Mildred NesSmith, Waurika, Oklahoma

1 *cup canned pineapple chunks with juice*
1 *banana, sliced*
1 *unpeeled Red Delicious apple, chopped*
3 *cups shredded lettuce*
¼ *cup crushed pecans*
2 *tablespoons mayonnaise*
1 *teaspoon granulated sugar*
  dash salt
2 *tablespoons Cool Whip*

Drain pineapple, reserving 1 tablespoon juice. Combine banana, apple, pineapple, lettuce, and pecans in a medium bowl.

Add mayonnaise, sugar, salt, Cool Whip, and pineapple juice. Toss well. Serves 6.

Vegetable Medley

Jan Hawkins, Nashville, Tennessee

Salad
1 *head cauliflower, washed, drained, and chopped into bite-size pieces*
1 *bunch broccoli, washed, drained, and chopped into bite-size pieces*
1 *2-ounce jar pimentos, drained and chopped*
1 *medium red onion, diced*
1 *medium green pepper, chopped into bite-size pieces*
2 *stalks celery, diced*
1 *large tomato, quartered*

Dressing
1 *cup mayonnaise*
¼ *cup granulated sugar*
¼ *cup vegetable oil*
2 *tablespoons celery seed*
2 *tablespoons dried chopped chives*

In a very large bowl, mix vegetables together.

In a small bowl, mix dressing ingredients together and add to vegetables. Toss well to distribute dressing evenly. Will stay fresh for a week if refrigerated. Serves 6.

Winter Salad

Mrs. Joseph Kowal, New London NSB, Connecticut

2 *large apples, cut into ½-inch pieces*
lemon juice
1 *small green cabbage, cut into ½-inch wedges*
½ *cup raisins*
½ *cup mayonnaise*
½ *cup vanilla yogurt*

Combine apples, cabbage, and raisins in a medium bowl. (If salad is not to be served immediately, mix apple pieces with a small amount of lemon juice to keep them from turning brown.)

Add mayonnaise and yogurt. Toss well. Serves 6.

Ground Beef

Austrian-Style Goulash
Lynn J. Catalina, Kirtland AFB, New Mexico

This Austrian recipe has been modified with extra meat and chopped potatoes.

   3 tablespoons vegetable oil
   3 medium onions, chopped
   2 cloves garlic, chopped
1½ pounds ground beef
   2 quarts beef stock or bouillon
   1 large bay leaf
   2 tablespoons chopped parsley
   3 16-ounce cans whole tomatoes, crushed
   1 green or yellow pepper, chopped
   3 large potatoes, diced
   1 tablespoon dried marjoram
     juice of 1 lemon
     salt and pepper to taste
1–2 tablespoons cornstarch (optional)

In a large stewpot, heat the oil and add onions and garlic. Sauté over medium-high heat until tender. Add meat and brown.

Add all ingredients except cornstarch, and simmer, covered, for 1 hour.

For thicker goulash, add cornstarch mixed with a little water and cook a few minutes more. Serves 6.

Aztec Rice

Mrs. Lea M. Wiltenmuth, Seattle, Washington

1½ cups uncooked white rice
1 tablespoon vegetable oil
1 pound lean ground beef
½ medium onion, chopped
¼ teaspoon garlic powder
1 15-ounce can stewed tomatoes
1 8-ounce can tomato sauce
1 4-ounce can diced green chiles
¼ teaspoon chili powder
¼ cup Burgundy or Marsala
    wine
1 cup water

Brown rice in oil in a medium saucepan. In a separate pan, fry ground beef, onion, and garlic powder until meat is browned. Do not drain off excess fat. Add meat mixture to the rice. Add tomatoes and sauce, drained chilies, chili powder, wine, and water.

Bring to a boil on high, then lower heat. Cover and cook for 20 minutes.

Let stand for 10 minutes before serving. Serves 6.

Beef and Potato Pie

Evette Binyard, Shaw AFB, South Carolina

    6 medium potatoes, peeled and chopped
    1 pound ground beef
    1 16-ounce can tomato puree
    1 sweet red pepper, chopped
    1 green pepper, chopped
    2 carrots, chopped
    1 medium onion, chopped
    ½ teaspoon salt
    ½ teaspoon pepper
    1½ cups water
    2 tablespoons butter
    ½ cup shredded cheddar cheese

Bring water to boil in a large saucepan. Add potatoes and boil until tender.

Meanwhile, brown ground beef in large skillet. Drain excess oil. Add tomato puree, peppers, carrots, onion, and seasonings. Add water and stir well. Simmer for 10 minutes.

When potatoes are done, drain and mash with butter. Set aside.

Put ground beef mixture into an 8 x 12-inch ungreased casserole dish. Top with mashed potatoes. Sprinkle with cheese. Bake, covered, in preheated oven at 350°F for 40 minutes. Uncover and bake for an additional 20 minutes, or until potatoes are golden brown. Serves 6.

Canadian Calico Beans

Doris Blind, Bremerton, Washington

½ *pound bacon, chopped*
1 *pound ground beef*
1 *cup chopped onions*
1 *1-pound can lima beans, drained*
1 *1-pound can kidney beans, drained*
1 *1-pound can pork and beans, drained*
1 *teaspoon dry mustard*
½ *cup ketchup*
¼ *cup molasses*
   chili powder to taste

In a medium skillet, brown the bacon until crisp. Drain.

Brown the ground beef in the same skillet and drain if necessary. Combine the bacon, ground beef, and onions with the remaining ingredients. Turn into an ungreased 9 x 13-inch casserole dish.

Bake, uncovered, in a preheated 350°F oven for 40 minutes. Serves 10.

Cattle Chatter Hash

Vickie L. Brown, NAS Moffett Field, California

2 tablespoons vegetable oil
1 pound ground beef
1 medium onion, chopped
2 tablespoons chili powder
1 teaspoon salt
1 8-ounce can tomato sauce
1 6-ounce package macaroni, cooked and drained according to package
   directions
1 10¾-ounce can condensed cream of mushroom soup
½ pound cheddar cheese, grated

In a medium skillet, heat the oil and brown the beef and onion until onion is tender. Add chili powder, salt, and tomato sauce. Stir well. Cover and simmer on low for 20 minutes.

Add macaroni and soup. Combine well. Turn into a 12-inch casserole dish. Top with cheese.

Bake in a preheated oven at 350°F for 30–40 minutes or until bubbly. Serves 6.

Chili Burritos

Hilda Lee Luckie, Fort Huachuca, Arizona

½ *pound ground beef*
½ *pound ground pork*
½ *pound chili meat*
1 *small onion, chopped*
1 *small clove garlic, chopped*
  salt and pepper to taste
⅓ *cup salsa*
½ *teaspoon dried basil, crushed*
½ *teaspoon dried tarragon, crushed*
1 *teaspoon chili powder*
2 *16-ounce cans refried beans*
12 *large flour tortillas*

In a large stewpot, combine all meats and brown over high heat until done. Stir often. Add onion, garlic, salt, and pepper. Cook over medium-high heat until vegetables are tender, stirring often.

Add remaining ingredients, except tortillas, and stir well. Simmer, uncovered, over low heat for 30 minutes. Add a touch of water if mixture gets too dry.

Warm tortillas in oven or on griddle. In the center of each tortilla, place ¼ cup ground meat mixture. Roll up and serve. Can be wrapped in aluminum foil and frozen. Makes 12.

Green Chili Casserole

Mrs. Dennis Martinez, Long Beach NB, California

    1 pound ground beef
    1 onion, finely chopped
    1 7-ounce can chopped green chilies, undrained
    2 10¾-ounce cans condensed cream of chicken soup
    6 large flour tortillas
    2 cups shredded cheddar cheese

Brown ground beef and onion in large skillet over medium-high heat. Drain off grease.

Add chilies and soup. Simmer 15 minutes, stirring occasionally.

Line an 8 x 12-inch casserole dish with 3 tortillas. Add half the meat mixture, then half the cheese. Cover with remaining tortillas, ground beef, and cheese, in that order.

Bake, uncovered, in a preheated oven at 350°F, for 10 minutes or until cheese is bubbly. Serves 6.

Hamburger Pizza

Mrs. Edwin Stonerock, Sr., Fort Sill, Oklahoma

1 pound ground beef
⅔ cup evaporated milk
½ cup bread crumbs
1 teaspoon garlic salt
1 6-ounce can tomato paste
1 3-ounce can sliced mushrooms, drained
1 cup shredded cheddar cheese
½ teaspoon oregano
2 tablespoons Parmesan cheese

Place meat, milk, bread crumbs, and garlic salt in a 9-inch pie pan. Mix thoroughly with a fork. Pat this mixture evenly in the bottom and up the sides of the pan. Press firmly in place.

Spread the tomato paste on top of the meat mixture. Arrange mushrooms on top of tomato paste. Top with shredded cheese. Sprinkle oregano and Parmesan cheese on top.

Bake, uncovered, in a preheated oven at 375°F for 25 minutes or until meat is done and cheese is browned. Serves 4.

Jacki's Chili

Carol Z. Hagen, Patuxent River NAS, Maryland

This chili is best made 24 hours in advance and reheated.

> 1½ *pounds ground beef*
> 8 *slices bacon*
> 1 *onion, chopped*
> 3 *15-ounce cans whole tomatoes, crushed*
> 1 *cup red wine*
> 1 *small jalapeno pepper*
> ½ *cup Worcestershire sauce*
> 1 *tablespoon chili powder*
> 1 *teaspoon dry mustard*
>   *salt and pepper to taste*
> 1 *15-ounce can kidney beans, drained*
> 1 *15-ounce can garbanzo beans, drained*

Brown the beef, bacon, and onion in a large stewpot. Drain excess fat.

Add the next 7 ingredients and combine well. Simmer, covered, 1–3 hours.

Add the kidney and garbanzo beans and cook until hot, about 10 minutes. Serves 10.

Meat Loaf Roll

Shelly Tebo, Norfolk NAS, Virginia

1 10-ounce package frozen chopped broccoli, unthawed
2 pounds ground beef
2 eggs
¾ cup bread crumbs
¼ cup ketchup
¼ cup milk
½ teaspoon salt
¼ teaspoon pepper
¼ teaspoon oregano
1 3-ounce package sliced smoked ham
3 3 x 3 x ¼-inch slices mozzarella cheese

Place frozen broccoli under running cold water to separate. Drain.

Mix ground beef, eggs, bread crumbs, ketchup, milk, salt, pepper, and oregano. Pat mixture into a rectangle, 10 x 12 inches, on a 15 x 18-inch piece of aluminum foil.

Arrange broccoli on top of meat to within ½ inch of edge. Arrange ham on broccoli.

Roll up rectangle carefully, beginning at the 10-inch side, using a fork to lift. Press edges and ends of hamburger roll to seal.

Place on rack in shallow roasting pan. Bake, uncovered, in a preheated oven at 350°F for 1¼ hours.

Overlap cheese on top and return to oven until cheese melts, about 1 minute. Serves 8.

Sloppy Mikes

Michael Hofmann, San Francisco, California

   3 *tablespoons vegetable oil*
   4 *potatoes, sliced paper-thin*
   1 *pound ground beef*
   1 *onion, chopped*
   1 *clove garlic, minced*
  ½ *teaspoon oregano*
  ¼ *teaspoon salt*
   1 *10-ounce package frozen spinach, thawed*
   2 *eggs, well beaten*

Cover the bottom of a medium skillet with oil and heat. Add the potatoes and cover. Cook over medium heat until just tender, about 10 minutes. Stir occasionally.

In a large skillet, brown the ground beef with the onion, garlic, oregano, and salt. Drain excess grease.

Add potatoes to the meat mixture. Add spinach and stir well. Cover and cook an additional 10 minutes. Add eggs, stirring constantly until eggs are set. Serve with ketchup, if desired. Serves 4.

The Tully Special
Mary E. Firment, Fort Campbell, Kentucky

1 *pound lean ground beef*
1 *tablespoon vegetable oil*
1 *16-ounce can tomato sauce*
6 *medium potatoes, sliced paper-thin*
1 *medium onion, chopped*
1 *medium green pepper, sliced into strips*
1 *medium zucchini, sliced thin*
  salt and pepper to taste

Brown the ground beef in oil until meat is slightly pink in color. Drain excess fat.

Layer the bottom of a 9-inch-square casserole dish with a small portion of tomato sauce. Add a layer of potatoes, then onion, green pepper, zucchini, meat, and seasonings. Continue layering until all ingredients are used, ending with a layer of tomato sauce.

Bake, covered, in a preheated oven at 425°F for 1 to 1½ hours or until vegetables are tender. Serves 6.

Your Fried Rice

Lonnie Jo Peterson, Holloman AFB, New Mexico

1 *pound 80% lean ground beef*
1 *cup chopped celery*
1 *cup chopped green onions*
1 *cup sliced mushrooms*
1 *cup diced carrots*
1 *10-ounce package frozen peas, unthawed*
1 *cup water*
4 *cups cooked rice*
   dash M.S.G.
½ *cup soy sauce, or to taste*
4 *eggs, scrambled*

In a large skillet, brown the ground beef. Do not drain.

Add vegetables and water, cover, and cook over medium heat for 10 minutes. Stir and cook another 5 minutes. Remove excess water.

Add rice, M.S.G., and soy sauce to taste. Heat thoroughly and then add eggs. Toss together and serve. Serves 6.

Meat

Beef Jerky

Gen Nilsen, Cerritos, California

1½ boneless beef brisket, semifrozen
¼ cup soy sauce
2 tablespoons Worchestershire sauce
3 teaspoons chopped onion
3 cloves garlic, pressed
1½ tablespoons brown sugar
½ teaspoon black pepper
¼ teaspoon ground ginger
½ teaspoon M.S.G.
dash nutmeg
1 teaspoon lemon pepper

While meat is still semifrozen, cut into thin strips across the grain.
Mix all ingredients except meat in a small bowl.

Place meat in a glass baking dish. Pour marinade over and refrigerate, covered, overnight, turning once.

Place meat on broiler pan and bake at 140°F to 160°F 8 hours.
Leave oven door propped open slightly.

Drain strips on paper towel and allow to dry. Store in zip-lock plastic bags. Will keep up to 6 months. Serves 6.

Bulgoki

Pat Hoffman, Seoul, Korea

This popular Korean dish is traditionally cooked at the table.

  1 *tablespoon granulated sugar*
  2 *green onions, chopped*
  3 *cloves garlic, sliced thin*
  3 *tablespoons sesame seeds*
  2 *teaspoons sesame oil*
  2 *tablespoons soy sauce*
  2 *small yellow onions*
  1 *teaspoon whiskey*
  1 *pound flank or round steak, sliced paper-thin*

In a large glass bowl, combine all ingredients except meat. Mix well. Add meat and combine thoroughly. Cover and refrigerate at least 3 hours.

Turn entire mixture into a large heated, ungreased skillet. Fry on high, stirring frequently, until onion is wilted, about 12 minutes. Serve over rice. Serves 3.

Easy Stroganoff

Kimberlee Breuer, Barksdale AFB, Louisiana

¼ cup butter or margarine
1 pound round steak, cut into 1-inch strips
½ cup chopped onion
⅓ cup chopped green pepper
⅓ cup chopped celery
1 4-ounce can sliced mushrooms, drained
salt and pepper to taste
½ teaspoon garlic powder
1 8-ounce package cream cheese
1 8-ounce container plain yogurt

Melt the butter or margarine in a large skillet and add the meat. Brown over medium-high heat for 2–3 minutes.

Add all the ingredients except cream cheese and yogurt. Cook for 5 minutes or until vegetables are tender.

Add the cream cheese and yogurt and cook, stirring, over low heat until smooth and warmed through. Serve over hot noodles or brown rice, if desired. Serves 4.

Flank Steak Essayons

Mrs. Charles R. Norris, Silver Spring, Maryland

½ cup olive oil
½ cup soy sauce
2 cloves garlic, pressed
1 lemon or lime, squeezed
1½ pounds flank steak
1 tablespoon chopped candied ginger

Combine all ingredients except steak in a long, shallow pan. Marinate steak in mixture for at least 4 hours, turning frequently. Barbecue 4–5 minutes per side over medium fire. To serve, slice meat on bias. Serves 4.

Fumie's Sukiyaki
Diana Dalla Betta, Camp Lejeune MCB, North Carolina

This meal is best made at the table, using an electric skillet. Small containers of soy sauce, beer, sugar, and water are placed around the skillet. The other ingredients are placed in a deep, large bowl. Cooking chopsticks are preferable to use for putting food in skillet, but you may use tongs.

½ cup beer
½ cup soy sauce
2 tablespoons granulated sugar
¾ cup water
1 small onion, chopped
1 pound top round steak or filet mignon, sliced into sandwich-thin
   strips, 2 inches long
1 large Chinese cabbage, chopped into 2-inch pieces
1 16-ounce can tofu, drained (may substitute fresh)
2 16-ounce cans yam threads (shirataki), drained
2 16-ounce cans bean sprouts, drained
   additional beer, soy sauce, sugar, and water

In an electric skillet, bring beer, soy sauce, sugar, and water to a boil.

Add onion and beef, cook until strips of beef are browned, and push to side.

Add cabbage and simmer a few minutes before adding tofu, yam threads, and bean sprouts. Cook until done, about 5–10 minutes. Add more beer, soy sauce, sugar, and water as needed. Serve with rice. Serves 4.

Hawaiian Pork Shoulder

SFC Doris Callender, Fitzsimons Army Medical Center,
Aurora, Colorado

1 *pork shoulder, about 4 pounds*
2 *4½-ounce jars strained peaches (baby food)*
¼ *cup soy sauce*
2 *cloves garlic, minced*
1 *teaspoon salt*
⅓ *cup ketchup*
⅓ *cup white or cider vinegar*
½ *cup dark brown sugar, firmly packed*
2 *teaspoons ground ginger*
  dash pepper

In a large roasting pan, bake pork in a preheated oven at 450°F for 15 minutes.

Meanwhile, combine remaining ingredients in a medium bowl. Stir well.

Remove pork from oven and trim fat. Return to pan and pour sauce over meat. Bake, uncovered, at 350°F for 1½ hours or until a meat thermometer registers done. Baste several times during baking. Serves 6.

Korean Fried Beef Strips

Evangelina Navarro, MacDill AFB, Florida

1 *pound top round steak, partially frozen*
2 *tablespoons vegetable oil*
2 *medium onions, thinly sliced*
1 *clove garlic, minced*
2 *green peppers, thinly sliced*
¼ *cup soy sauce*
1 *tomato, cut into wedges*

Thinly slice beef into bite-size strips.

In a wok or large skillet, heat oil, add onions, garlic, and green peppers. Cook over high heat until wilted, about 10 minutes, stirring often. Pour on soy sauce after 5 minutes.

Add the beef and cook until done to your taste. Add the tomato for the last 2 minutes. Stir often. Serve over rice. Serves 4.

Lamb Ratatouille

Melissa Nelson, Hunter Army Air Field, Georgia

1 *quart tomato sauce*
1 *tablespoon coriander leaves*
2 *pounds lamb stew cubes*
   salt and pepper to taste
¼ *cup dry vermouth*
2 *tablespoons lemon juice*
1 *small eggplant, cut into 1-inch cubes*
2 *green peppers, cut into 1-inch squares*
2 *medium zucchini, cut into ½-inch squares*
2 *medium onions, cut into ¼-inch slices*
½ *cup chicken stock*
1 *tablespoon olive oil*

Spoon tomato sauce into the bottom of a Dutch oven. Sprinkle with coriander leaves.

Place lamb cubes in sauce. Sprinkle with salt, pepper, vermouth, and lemon juice. Simmer, covered, over low heat for 2 hours.

One and a half hours before serving, salt the eggplant and place in a medium bowl. Fill with water.

One half hour before serving, drain eggplant. In a large skillet, put eggplant, peppers, zucchini, onions, and chicken stock. Bring to a boil, cover, and simmer for 30 minutes.

Arrange vegetables on a platter. Drizzle with olive oil. Arrange lamb and tomato mixture over vegetables. Serves 6.

Marinated London Broil

Teresa L. Hamernik, Ramstein AFB, West Germany

> 1 *pound London broil*
> ¾ *cup olive oil*
> ¼ *cup soy sauce*
> 2 *cloves garlic, crushed*
> ¼ *cup dry sherry (optional)*

Wipe meat on both sides with damp cloth and pierce all over with a fork.

Combine remaining ingredients in a 9 x 13 x 2-inch nonmetallic dish. Place meat in marinade. Cover and marinate at least 2 hours, turning frequently.

Preheat broiler or prepare charcoal grill. Remove meat from marinade and broil 8–12 minutes per side depending on personal taste. Brush frequently with marinade. Remove from grill, cut on the cross-grain and serve immediately. Serves 4.

Marinated Venison

Saloma Compton, Mountain Home AFB, Idaho

This marinade is great for fresh venison, but it also can be used for any other meat.

3 *tablespoons soy sauce*
1 *tablespoon brown sugar*
1 *tablespoon dark molasses*
1 *teaspoon finely chopped onion*
2 *teaspoons prepared mustard*
½ *teaspoon cornstarch*
¼ *teaspoon dried sage, crumbled*
1½ *pounds venison, cut into thin strips*
2 *tablespoons vegetable oil*

Combine all ingredients except meat and oil in a small bowl. Mix well.

Place meat in a large, shallow dish. Pour marinade over. Cover. Refrigerate overnight.

Heat oil in skillet and stir-fry meat on high heat until cooked through. Serves 4.

Mock Beef Stroganoff
Robin Stout, Fort Lee, Virginia

2 *pounds stew beef, cut into bite-size pieces*
1 *medium onion, chopped*
1 *10-ounce can condensed cream of mushroom soup*
1 *10-ounce can condensed cream of celery soup*
1 *10-ounce can condensed cream of chicken soup*

Place beef in crockpot. Add chopped onion and all soup. Stir and cover. Cook on medium all day, stirring once every hour. Serve over cooked noodles. Serves 8.

Orange Pork Steaks

Lonnie Jo Peterson, Holloman AFB, New Mexico

> 4 *pork steaks, 6–8 ounces each, about ½-inch thick*
> 1 *6-ounce can orange juice concentrate*
> 1½ *cans water*
> ¼ *cup Worcestershire sauce*
> 1 *orange, washed and sliced into thin slices*

In a large frying pan or electric skillet, fry the steaks for 2 minutes on each side.

Combine orange juice with water. Mix well. Add Worchestershire sauce and mix again.

Pour sauce over steaks and let simmer, covered, for 30 minutes.

To serve, put 2 orange slices on each steak for a garnish. Serve with rice. Serves 4.

Roast Leg of Lamb
Gail Trafelet, Bowie, Maryland

Have your butcher remove the bone to make the leg of lamb easier to carve.

> 1 *5-pound leg of lamb*
> 1½ *teaspoon salt*
> 1 *clove garlic, thinly sliced*
> *pepper to taste*
> ¼ *cup melted butter or margarine*
> 3 *tablespoons lemon juice*
> ⅔ *cup dry white wine*

Wipe leg of lamb with damp towel and make 8–10 gashes in it. Sprinkle holes with salt and rub in. Place a garlic sliver in each gash. Grind pepper over whole surface and rub in.

Place leg in roasting pan. Combine melted butter or margarine and lemon juice and pour over meat. Pour wine over meat.

Bake in a preheated oven at 325°F for 25 minutes per pound or until done to your liking as indicated on a meat thermometer. Baste frequently with pan juices.

When done, let stand a few minutes before carving. Slice thin and serve with pan juices. Serves 10.

Rolled Beef

Linda Benson, Fort Gillem, Georgia

If placed in an airtight container, rolled beef keeps up to three months in the freezer without losing its flavor.

> 1 *3–4 pound round roast, trimmed*
> ¼ *cup Dijon-style mustard (approximately)*
> ½ *pound bacon, sliced in half*
> 2 *medium onions, 1 chopped, 1 quartered*
> 1 *8-ounce jar dill pickles, sliced thin lengthwise*
> 1 *quart water*
> 1 *28-ounce can whole canned tomatoes,*
>   *crushed*
> 4 *bay leaves*
> 5 *beef bouillon cubes*
> ¼ *cup corn starch*
> ¼ *cup water*

Turn roast lengthwise and slice into ⅛-inch slices approximately 6 inches long by 4 inches wide. Place beef slices, one by one, between sheets of waxed paper and pound with a rolling pin to flatten. Do not puncture.

Spread each slice with 1 teaspoon mustard. Place ½ slice bacon, 1 tablespoon chopped onion and 3 pickle slices on each slice.

Roll meat up and secure with toothpicks or string.

Place meat in hot Dutch oven and brown on all sides. Add quart of water and let simmer, uncovered, for 1 hour.

Add tomatoes, quartered onion, bay leaves, and bouillon cubes. Cover and simmer for another hour.

Remove meat from pan. Set aside. Pour liquid through cheesecloth or strainer into large bowl. Press through as much pulp and liquid as possible. Discard solids. Return liquid to pan and bring to boil.

Mix cornstarch with ¼ cup water. Add to liquid to thicken. Add water if necessary to reach desired consistency.

Reduce heat to simmer and return meat to pan. Simmer for 1½ hours. Serves 8.

Scraps Deluxe

Mrs. Susanne Hart, Giessen, West Germany

3 tablespoons butter or margarine
½ pound sirloin, sliced thin
½ pound boneless pork loin, sliced thin
1 onion, cut into rings
½ green pepper, sliced
½ sweet red pepper, sliced
1 large tomato, chunked
½ cup beef broth
1 12-ounce can sliced mushrooms, drained
2 tablespoons tomato paste
1 tablespoon sour cream
2 tablespoons white wine

Melt butter or margarine in skillet over medium-high heat. Add meat, brown quickly on both sides. Remove to a platter and keep warm.

Sauté the onion, peppers, and tomato chunks in the same skillet until tender. Stir in broth and simmer 2–3 minutes.

Return meat to skillet. Add mushrooms, tomato paste, sour cream, and wine. Heat thoroughly but do not boil. Serve over rice. Serves 4.

The oldest building at Camp Pendleton, California, the Ranch House Chapel once housed a winery for the Mission San Luis Rey. In later years it belonged to the prosperous Rancho Santa Margarita y Las Flores. Built of adobe in the typical Spanish architectural style with a red tile roof, the chapel is on the National Register of Historic Landmarks. *Drawing by Sgt. Art Alejandre, courtesy of Camp Pendleton.*

Poultry

Adela's Chicken
Adela Hernandez, Norton AFB, California

This Cuban recipe traditionally is eaten with rice and fried plantains.

 3 *tablespoons vegetable oil*
 1 *pound boneless chicken breasts, skinned and cut into 2-inch chunks*
 1 *cup chopped onion*
 1 *cup chopped green pepper*
 1 *clove garlic, chopped*
 2 *cups water*
 3 *chicken bouillon cubes*
 3 *ounces tomato sauce*
 1 *teaspoon ground cumin*
 3 *bay leaves*

Heat oil in large skillet and add chicken, onion, green pepper, and garlic. Sauté over medium-high heat until chicken is lightly browned and vegetables are tender.

Add water, bouillon cubes, tomato sauce, and spices. Bring to a boil. Reduce heat and simmer, covered, for 30–40 minutes or until chicken is tender. Remove bay leaves before serving. Serve over rice, if desired. Serves 4.

Chicken Breasts Supreme

Mrs. Joseph Kowal, Norwich, Connecticut

½ cup chopped onion
½ pound mushrooms
2 tablespoons butter or margarine
2 10-ounce packages frozen chopped broccoli, thawed
6 strips cooked bacon, diced
¼ cup grated Parmesan cheese
1 cup bread crumbs
1 teaspoon dried parsley
½ teaspoon garlic powder
½ teaspoon poultry seasoning
   salt and pepper to taste
4 half boneless chicken breasts

Cheese Sauce
1½ tablespoons butter
1½ tablespoons flour
¾ cup milk
½ cup shredded cheddar cheese
½ teaspoon salt

In a medium skillet, sauté the onions and mushrooms in butter or margarine until almost tender.

Mix all ingredients except chicken together in a large mixing bowl. Place in 4 individual 1½-cup casserole dishes.

Mold chicken over stuffing. Bake, covered, in a preheated oven at 350°F for 45–55 minutes or until chicken is tender.

In a medium saucepan, melt the butter over medium-low heat. Whisk in the flour until smooth. Whisk in the milk. When sauce is smooth and thickened, stir in the cheese and salt. Stir until cheese is melted.

Remove chicken from oven and top with cheese sauce. Serve immediately. Serves 4.

Chicken in Red Wine
Cynthia Cox, Camp Pendleton, California

This recipe can be made with rabbit instead of chicken.

¼ *pound bacon, diced*
1 *cup chopped onion*
¼ *pound mushrooms, sliced*
¼ *cup butter or margarine, divided*
2 *broiler-fryers, about 3½ pounds each, cut up, washed and dried*
1 *bay leaf*
½ *teaspoon dried tarragon*
4 *peppercorns*
1 *teaspoon salt*
2 *cups red wine*
1 *tablespoon all-purpose flour*
2 *tablespoons chopped fresh parsley*

Cook bacon in a Dutch oven until crispy. Remove bacon and set aside. Add onion and mushrooms to bacon grease. Cook until tender. Remove and reserve.

Melt 3 tablespoons butter or margarine in pan. Add chicken, bay leaf, tarragon, and peppercorns. Cook until chicken is lightly browned, about 5 minutes.

Combine salt and wine. Pour over chicken. Bring to a boil, reduce heat, and simmer, covered, for 25 minutes or until chicken is tender.

In a small bowl, combine flour and remaining 1 tablespoon butter or margarine. Add a bit of hot liquid to flour and then pour flour mixture into pan. Stir to thicken sauce. Add parsley and serve. Serves 8.

Chicken Ketch-A-Tori

Colette Iusi, Aurora, Colorado

6 *half chicken breasts*
2 *tablespoons olive oil*
2 *medium onions, sliced in rings*
½ *pound mushrooms, sliced*
2 *medium green peppers, sliced in rings*
2 *cloves garlic, crushed*
1 *12-ounce can tomato paste*
2 *cups ketchup*
¾ *cup water*
2 *teaspoons onion salt*
1 *teaspoon dried oregano*
¼ *cup dried parsley*

Rinse chicken. In a large skillet, heat oil and brown the chicken breasts until golden.

Place breasts in the bottom of a large Dutch oven. Place the onions, mushrooms, and green peppers on top.

In a medium bowl, combine the remaining ingredients and mix well. Pour this mixture over the chicken and vegetables.

Bake, covered, in preheated oven at 350°F for 1½ to 2 hours. Serve over mashed potatoes. Serves 6.

Chicken Marsala

Marie Marchesini, Bedford, Massachusetts

>   3 *whole boneless chicken breasts*
>   1 *egg, beaten*
>   ¼ *cup milk*
>   1 *cup flour (approximately)*
>   1½ *teaspoons salt*
>   ¼ *teaspoon pepper*
>   3 *tablespoons oil*
>   3 *tablespoons butter*
>   2 *green peppers, cut into matchstick strips*
>   1 *small onion, chopped*
>   ½ *pound mushrooms (sliced if large)*
>   1 *clove garlic, minced*
>   1 *cup Marsala wine*
>   1 *cup chicken broth*

Flatten chicken between sheets of wax paper with a rolling pin or mallet.

Combine egg and milk in a shallow dish. Combine flour, salt, and pepper in another shallow dish.

Dip chicken into egg mixture and then flour mixture to coat all over. Refrigerate chicken pieces 2–3 hours.

Heat oil and butter in a large skillet. Brown chicken on both sides and remove to plate. In the same skillet, sauté green peppers, onions, mushrooms, and garlic until tender. Remove to platter.

Add wine and chicken broth. Simmer, uncovered, until liquid is reduced by half.

Return chicken and vegetables to pan and heat through. Arrange on serving platter. Serves 6.

Chicken 'n' Wine

Mayra A. Martinez, Fort Jackson, South Carolina

1 *large egg*
¼ *cup grated Parmesan cheese*
2 *whole boneless chicken breasts*
2 *tablespoons butter or margarine*
½ *cup dry white wine*
  salt and pepper to taste

In a medium bowl, beat the egg and add the Parmesan cheese.

Cut the chicken breasts into 2-inch cubes. Add the chicken to the cheese and egg mixture. Combine well.

In a large skillet, melt the butter or margarine. Add the chicken and cook over medium-high heat 5 minutes. Stir often.

Add wine, salt, and pepper to skillet. Cover and reduce heat. Cook on low for 15 minutes. Uncover, and simmer 5 minutes to reduce liquid. Serve with rice, if desired. Serves 4.

Chicken Salad

Saloma Compton, Mountain Home AFB, Idaho

    1 *head lettuce, torn into bite-size pieces*
    ½ *cup chopped purple cabbage*
    1 *carrot, peeled and grated*
    1 *tomato, cut into wedges*
    1 *6¾-ounce can chunk chicken*
    ¾ *cup Italian dressing*

Combine lettuce, cabbage, carrot, and tomato in a large salad bowl. Drain chicken thoroughly and add it to bowl. Pass the dressing at the table. Serves 4.

Chicken Scallopine with Lemon Zest
Jenny Bretana, Pirmasens, West Germany

4 *half boneless chicken breasts*
½ *tablespoon salt*
¼ *teaspoon pepper*
 flour for dredging
½ *lemon*
1 *tablespoon vegetable oil*
1 *tablespoon butter or margarine*
½ *teaspoon dried rosemary, crushed*
1 *large garlic clove, crushed*
¼ *cup dry white wine*
½ *cup chicken broth*
½ *cup sour cream*

Pound chicken with a mallet until each half breast is ¼-inch thick. Sprinkle each with salt and pepper.

In a small bowl, place enough flour to coat all the chicken. Dip each breast in the flour and pat briskly to remove the excess.

Remove rind from the lemon with a potato peeler. Be careful to remove the yellow part only, not the white pulp. Stack strips on a chopping board and cut crosswise into fine julienne strips.

Heat the oil and butter or margarine in a large skillet. On medium-high heat, sauté chicken until golden brown on both sides, about 5 minutes total. Sprinkle the rosemary and garlic over the chicken and shake the pan to distribute evenly. Add the wine and chicken broth. Cook, uncovered, over medium heat, until the pan liquid is reduced by a third.

Remove chicken to a warm platter. Turn the heat under the skillet to low. Stir in the sour cream and half the lemon rind. Heat slowly but do not allow to boil. When sauce is warmed through, pour it over the chicken and sprinkle with remaining lemon rind. Serves 4.

Chicken with Coconut

Lola Anderson, Redondo Beach, California

This Guamanian recipe is traditionally served on holidays, including Christmas and Easter, and for other family gatherings.

> 3 *half boneless chicken breasts*
> ¼ *cup lemon juice*
> ¼ *teaspoon salt*
> ¼ *teaspoon black pepper*
> 3 *green onions, chopped fine*
> 1 *stalk celery, diced*
> 1 *fresh yellow chili or jalapeno pepper, diced fine*
> ½ *coconut, grated (about 1 cup)*

Broil chicken until done but not dry. Dice cooked chicken into pea-size pieces.

In a medium bowl, combine the chicken, lemon juice, salt, pepper, onions, celery, and chili. Then add coconut. Serve immediately. Serves 4.

Chili Chicken

Marie Coley Schersching, Langley AFB, Virginia

1 *broiler-fryer, about 2½ pounds*
2 *tablespoons vegetable oil*
4 *small zucchini, sliced*
6 *medium jalapeno peppers, diced fine*
1 *medium onion, chopped*
1 *clove garlic, minced*
1 *10¾-ounce can condensed cream of mushroom soup*
1 *10-ounce package frozen corn*
  salt and pepper to taste
1 *pint sour cream*
1 *8-ounce package corn chips*
2 *cups shredded Monterey Jack cheese*
  paprika and additional jalapenos for garnish

Rinse chicken and place with giblets in 2 inches of water in a 4-quart saucepan. Bring to a boil, reduce heat and simmer, covered, for 35 minutes. Remove from heat and cool until easy to handle. Reserve broth and giblets for another meal. Bone and cut chicken into bite-size pieces. Set aside.

In a large skillet, heat oil and add zucchini, peppers, onion, and garlic. Fry until tender, stirring occasionally. Add soup, corn, salt, and pepper. Bring to a boil over high heat. Stir in chicken and sour cream and heat through. Remove from heat.

In a 2-quart casserole, arrange one-third of the corn chips. Top with one-third of the cheese and then half of the chicken mixture. Repeat, ending with cheese. Bake, uncovered, in a preheated oven at 350°F for 30 minutes or until heated through. Sprinkle with paprika and garnish with jalapeno peppers, if desired.

Cindy's Oriental Chicken
Cindy Shaffer, White Sands Missile Range, New Mexico

2 eggs, beaten
1¼ cups ice water
1½ cups all-purpose flour
1½ pounds boneless chicken, skinned and cut into 1-inch cubes
¼ cup sesame oil
⅓ cup peanut oil
3 large carrots, sliced thin
2 stalks celery, chopped fine
4 green onions, chopped fine
1 green pepper, chopped
1 zucchini, sliced thin
1 5-ounce can bamboo shoots, drained
⅓ cup honey
¼ cup soy sauce
2 tablespoons red wine vinegar
2 teaspoons garlic powder
1½ teaspoons ground ginger
1 tablespoon all-purpose flour

Mix eggs, water, and the 1½ cups flour together in a medium bowl to make a batter. Batter will be lumpy. Dip chicken pieces in batter, coating each completely.

Heat the oils in a large skillet or wok. Fry chicken in the oil over medium-high heat, turning once, until lightly browned. Remove chicken to paper-towel-lined dish. Reserve 2 tablespoons oil in pan.

In the reserved oil, stir-fry carrots, celery, and green onions for 5 minutes over medium-high heat. Add remaining vegetables and fry an additional 3 minutes or until wilted.

While vegetables are cooking, mix together honey, soy sauce, vinegar, garlic powder, ginger, and 1 tablespoon flour. Add to vegetable mixture and cook until thickened.

Return chicken to pan and heat thoroughly. Serve over rice, if desired. Serves 6.

Cola Chicken

Mrs. Angela J. Adams, Lilburn, Georgia

1 2½-pound fryer, cut up
1 cup Classic Coke
1½ cups ketchup
2 cups water
   dash salt

Place all ingredients in a Dutch oven and bring to a boil over high heat. Reduce heat and simmer gently for 1 hour, uncovered, or until chicken is tender and sauce has thickened. Serve chicken and sauce over hot rice. Serves 4.

Downright Perfect Fried Chicken
Laura Draper, Atoka, Tennessee

1 cup all-purpose flour
½ cup bread crumbs
1 teaspoon garlic powder
1 teaspoon parsley
½ cup grated Parmesan cheese
2 eggs, beaten
¼ cup water
1 3-pound fryer, cut up
2 cups vegetable oil

Mix all dry ingredients in one large, shallow bowl. In another shallow bowl, beat eggs and water together. Dip each piece of chicken in egg mixture and then in flour mixture.

Heat oil in large frying pan until very hot. Turn down heat to medium-low and place chicken in the pan. Keep turning the chicken until oil cools down a little.

Cover and cook for 25–30 minutes, turning pieces occasionally.

Turn heat to high to recrisp the chicken, then remove and place on a paper-towel-lined plate. Serves 4.

Easy Chicken Dijon
Diana L. Reynolds, Port Hueneme CBC, California

1 *2-pound fryer, cut up*
¼ *cup Dijon-style mustard*
½ *cup bread crumbs*
¼ *cup water or dry white wine*
2 *tablespoons dried thyme*
2 *teaspoons dried or finely chopped fresh parsley*
   pepper to taste

Brush chicken pieces with mustard. Roll in bread crumbs. Place chicken in ungreased 9 x 13-inch baking dish.

Sprinkle water or wine over each piece. Scatter crushed herbs over chicken. Sprinkle pepper over all.

Bake, uncovered, in a preheated oven at 350°F for 30 minutes. Serves 4.

Easy Sweet and Sour Chicken
Mary Herkert, Kittery, Maine

1 *3-pound fryer, cut up, or 3 pounds of wings*
1 *10-ounce bottle Russian salad dressing*
1 *8-ounce jar apricot or peach jam*
1 *envelope dry onion soup mix*
2 *tablespoons water*

Place chicken in 9 x 12-inch ungreased baking dish.

In a small bowl, combine remaining ingredients. Mix well.

Pour jam mixture over chicken, coating completely. Bake, uncovered, in preheated oven at 350°F for 30–40 minutes. Baste with pan juices at least once. Serves 6.

Mexican Chicken

Patricia Ann Novak, Schwabish Gmund, West Germany

1 *7-ounce bag nacho-flavored corn chips*
1 *chicken, boiled and deboned, or 4 cups cooked chicken*
1 *tablespoon butter or margarine*
½ *cup diced onion*
2 *10½-ounce cans condensed cream of chicken soup*
2 *7-ounce cans taco sauce*
2 *cups grated cheddar cheese*

Crush the chips with a rolling pin and put into a 9 x 13-inch baking pan. Place chicken over chips.

In a medium saucepan, melt butter or margarine and sauté onion until translucent. Add soup and taco sauce. Stir well. Bring to a boil and then pour over the chicken. Top with grated cheese.

Bake, uncovered, in preheated oven at 345°F for 30 minutes. Serves 4.

Ming Chicken

Louisa Otis, Sylt, West Germany

1 *whole 3-pound fryer, cut up and with skin removed*
¼ *cup vegetable oil*
¼ *cup honey*
4 *teaspoons Dijon-style mustard*
3 *tablespoons sesame seeds*
1 *teaspoon salt*

In a 12-inch ovenproof skillet, brown the chicken on all sides in hot oil. Remove from heat.

Combine honey, mustard, sesame seed, and salt. Spread half the mixture over chicken.

Bake, covered, in a preheated oven at 350°F for 30 minutes. Turn chicken and spread with remaining sauce. Cover pan and return to oven. Bake 30 minutes more or until chicken is tender. Serves 4.

Pineapple Chicken
Gail Guild, Vance AFB, Oklahoma

1½ *pounds cooked chicken, diced*
1 *cup diced celery*
1½ *tablespoons diced onion*
1 *20-ounce can diced pineapple, drained*
1 *cup mayonnaise*
½ *teaspoon pepper*
¼ *cup lemon juice*
1 *cup grated cheddar cheese*
  crushed potato chips to cover, about 1½ cups

In a large mixing bowl, toss together all ingredients except cheese and potato chips. Place in 9 x 13-inch baking pan. Sprinkle with cheese and top with potato chips.

Bake, uncovered, in preheated oven at 350°F for 30 minutes. Serves 10.

Ripe Olive Portuguese Chicken
Gail Trafelet, Bowie, Maryland

1 cup all-purpose flour
1 teaspoon salt
1¼ teaspoon pepper
1¼ 3-pound fryer, cut up
3 tablespoons vegetable oil
¼ cup chopped onion
1 clove garlic, minced
1 tablespoon flour
1 cup canned whole tomatoes, crushed
¼ cup water
1 chicken bouillon cube
1 cup ripe olives, cut in halves
2 medium tomatoes, cut in eighths
1 tablespoon chopped fresh parsley

Combine 1 cup flour, salt, and pepper in a shallow bowl. Coat chicken pieces in flour.

Heat oil in large stewpot and add chicken. Cook over medium-high heat until chicken is browned on both sides, about 10 minutes. Remove chicken from pan.

Sauté onion and garlic in the stewpot until transparent. Stir in the 1 tablespoon flour. Add canned tomatoes, water, and bouillon cube. Cook, stirring, until sauce boils and thickens.

Return chicken to pan. Cover tightly and cook over low heat for 30 minutes.

Add olives and cook, covered, for 10 more minutes. Add tomatoes and cook 5–10 minutes longer.

Place in serving dish and sprinkle with parsley. Serve over egg noodles, if desired. Serves 4.

RR's Chicken Delight

Jeanie Reed, Camp Lejeune, North Carolina

1 *pound boneless chicken breasts, skinned and cut into 1-inch strips*
⅓ *cup cornstarch*
¼ *cup vegetable oil*
1 *cup sliced green onions*
¼ *pound mushrooms, sliced*
¾ *cup chicken broth*
½ *cup heavy cream*
½ *teaspoon dried thyme*
1 *teaspoon dried tarragon*

Dredge each chicken piece in cornstarch. Heat oil in skillet. Add chicken and brown over high heat 2 minutes. Add green onions and mushrooms. Sauté 3 minutes or until tender.

Add chicken broth and bring to a boil. Turn down heat to low, stir in cream, thyme, and tarragon. Simmer 5 minutes. Serve over rice, if desired. Serves 4.

Stir-Fried Chicken and Mushrooms

Susan Stanioch, Fort McClellan, Alabama

2 *whole chicken breasts, skinned, boned and cut into ⅛-inch slices*
2 *tablespoons soy sauce*
2 *tablespoons dry sherry*
2 *tablespoons cornstarch*
1 *teaspoon minced fresh ginger or ¼ teaspoon ground ginger*
¼ *teaspoon granulated sugar*
¼ *teaspoon garlic powder*
¼ *cup plus 3 tablespoons vegetable oil, divided*
1 *pound mushrooms, sliced thin*
4 *green onions, cut in thirds*
1 *cup frozen peas, thawed*

In a medium bowl, combine chicken, soy sauce, sherry, cornstarch, ginger, sugar, and garlic powder. Mix well and set aside.

In large skillet or wok, heat ¼ cup oil over medium-high heat. Add mushrooms and green onions, stirring quickly and frequently until mushrooms are tender, about 2 minutes. Remove mushroom mixture and set aside.

Add remaining oil to pan and cook chicken over high heat, stirring quickly and frequently until chicken is tender, about 2–3 minutes. Return mushroom mixture to pan. Add peas. Heat through. Serve over rice, if desired. Serves 4.

Turkey Oriental

Arlene Kooman, Visalia, California

> 5 teaspoons butter or margarine
> 1 medium onion, sliced
> 1 green pepper, sliced
> 2 stalks celery, sliced
> 1 1-pound can bean sprouts, undrained
> 1 3-ounce can sliced mushrooms, drained
> 1 5¼-ounce can bamboo shoots, drained
> 1½ cups cooked turkey, cut into strips
> 2 tablespoons cornstarch
> ⅓ cup water
> 5 teaspoons soy sauce

Heat butter or margarine in a large skillet. Add onion, pepper, and celery. Sauté until tender. Add bean sprouts with their liquid, mushrooms, bamboo shoots, and turkey.

Cover and cook over low heat 15 minutes.

In a small bowl, combine cornstarch, water, and soy sauce, mixing until smooth. Stir cornstarch mixture into turkey. Continue cooking until mixture thickens.

Serve over rice. Serves 6.

Seafood

Bombay Shrimp

Jean P. Klotzbach, Columbia, Maryland

    1 10¾-ounce can condensed cream of chicken soup
 ½ to 1 teaspoon curry powder, to taste
        dash pepper
    1 cup evaporated milk
    2 cups shelled, deveined and cooked shrimp
   ¼ cup chopped salted peanuts

Combine soup, curry powder, pepper, and evaporated milk in a medium saucepan. Mix well until smooth, then simmer until hot, about 10 minutes.

Add shrimp and heat thoroughly, about 5 minutes. Top with peanuts and serve over rice. Serves 4.

Crabmeat-Stuffed Green Peppers

Jeanette Barnett, Las Vegas, Nevada

This Cajun dish is a favorite holiday dish in Louisiana.

> 6 *large green peppers*
> 2 *tablespoons cornstarch*
> ¼ *cup dry white wine*
> 1 *teaspoon lemon juice*
> 1 *teaspoon salt*
> 1 *cup light cream*
> ¼ *cup butter or margarine*
> ¼ *teaspoon ground nutmeg*
> 2 *cups cooked, shredded crabmeat*
> 1 *cup cooked rice*
> *paprika for garnish*

Cut tops off peppers and remove seeds. Parboil peppers in large pot for 5 minutes and then invert to remove all water.

In a small bowl, combine cornstarch, wine, lemon juice, and salt. Set aside.

In a medium saucepan, scald cream. Add butter or margarine, nutmeg, and cornstarch mixture. Cook on low heat until mixture is thick, stirring constantly. Add crabmeat and rice.

Spoon crabmeat mixture into peppers. Sprinkle with paprika. Place peppers in a greased 19 x 19 x 2-inch baking dish. Bake, uncovered, in a preheated oven at 350°F for 20 minutes or until bubbly. Serves 6.

Curried Shrimp and Potato Casserole
Marlene Weldon, Phoenix, Arizona

1 *cup sour cream*
1 *10½-ounce can condensed cream of shrimp soup*
1 *teaspoon curry powder*
1 *20-ounce package frozen shrimp*
1 *1-pound package frozen potato nuggets*
¼ *cup chopped green olives*
2 *tablespoons chopped black olives*
   mandarin oranges and slivered almonds for garnish (optional)

Combine sour cream, soup, and curry powder in a 2-quart casserole dish. Add shrimp, potato nuggets, and olives, and stir well.
Bake in a preheated oven at 350°F for 30 minutes or until bubbly. Remove from oven and garnish with mandarin oranges and almonds. Serve over chow mein noodles, if desired. Serves 6.

Fish Roll-Ups

Roxane Hildebrant, Coast Guard Station, Oswego, New York

6 fish fillets (about 2 pounds)
salt and paprika to taste
1 tablespoon butter or margarine
¼ cup chopped onion
1 clove garlic, minced
½ cup dry white wine
1 16-ounce can whole tomatoes, drained and cut up
1 teaspoon granulated sugar
2 teaspoons cornstarch
1 tablespoon cold water

Thaw fish if frozen. Sprinkle each fillet with salt and paprika. Roll up each and secure with a toothpick. Set aside.

In a large skillet, melt butter or margarine and sauté onion and garlic until tender. Do not brown. Add wine, tomatoes, and sugar. Bring to a boil, then add fish.

Cover and reduce heat to low. Simmer 15–20 minutes or until fish flakes easily. Remove fish to platter and keep warm.

Turn heat to high and boil liquid, uncovered, until it is reduced to about 1½ cups.

Combine cornstarch and water. Add to skillet. Stir constantly over high heat until mixture is thick and bubbly. Spoon sauce over fish and serve immediately. Serves 6.

Italian Shrimp

Melissa Nelson, Savannah, Georgia

½ cup olive oil
¾ teaspoon salt
¼ teaspoon pepper
½ teaspoon garlic powder
¼ cup minced parsley
1 tablespoon minced pimiento
2 pounds large shrimp, shelled and deveined
3 tablespoons butter
3 tablespoons lemon juice

In a medium bowl, combine oil, salt, pepper, garlic powder, parsley, and pimiento.

Dip each shrimp into this mixture and cook in a hot skillet over low heat about 2 minutes on each side. Spoon 2–3 tablespoons of oil mixture over shrimp. Cover and cook 5–8 minutes, turning once.

Transfer shrimp into a serving dish. Keep warm. Add butter and lemon juice to skillet. Stir and heat until mixture begins to sizzle. Pour over shrimp and serve immediately. Serves 4.

Nonie's Shrimp Tetrazini

Nonie Schoelles, Apalachicola, Florida

1 *pound small, uncooked shrimp*
½ *teaspoon salt*
1 *tablespoon grated onion*
 dash pepper
3 *tablespoons butter*
3 *tablespoons flour*
½ *teaspoon paprika*
½ *teaspoon oregano*
 Tabasco sauce to taste
¾ *cup milk*
1 *egg*
1 *3-ounce can mushrooms, undrained*
6 *ounces hot, cooked spaghetti*
3 *tablespoons grated Parmesan cheese*

In a medium saucepan, combine shrimp, salt, onion, and pepper. Add water to cover, about 1 cup. Cover and simmer 10 minutes.

Drain the shrimp mixture, reserving ¾ cup cooking liquid. Set the shrimp aside.

In the same saucepan, melt the butter and blend in flour, paprika, oregano, and Tabasco. Add reserved liquid and milk. Cook, stirring, until thickened.

In a small bowl, beat the egg and add a little of the thickened hot sauce. Stir. Return mixture to pan and mix well.

Add the undrained mushrooms and shrimp. Stir well.

Spoon the spaghetti into a 9 x 13-inch casserole dish. Top with shrimp mixture. Sprinkle with Parmesan cheese. Broil for 5 minutes or until cheese is browned and bubbly. Serves 4.

Pancit Bihon

Amy Naval, Warner Robins, Georgia

3 tablespoons vegetable oil
1 medium onion, sliced thin
2 cloves garlic, chopped
½ pound shrimp
1 pound chicken breasts cut into 1-inch strips
2 carrots, cut into thin strips
2 cups shredded green cabbage
1 pound Japanese or Chinese rice noodles, soaked in warm water for 15
  minutes and then drained
⅓ cup soy sauce
  pepper to taste
1 hardboiled egg, shelled and quartered for garnish
  chopped green onions for garnish

Heat the oil in a large skillet and sauté onion and garlic until tender.

Add shrimp, chicken, and carrots. Cook on high heat for 5 minutes, stirring constantly.

Add cabbage, noodles, soy sauce, and pepper, and cook for 10 minutes over medium-low heat. Add a few drops of water if mixture becomes too dry.

Turn into serving dish and garnish with egg and green onions. Serves 10.

Pimiento-Glazed Bass

Jeanie Reed, Camp Lejeune MCB, North Carolina

1½ *pounds bass, ocean perch, snapper, or other rock fish fillets*
1 *teaspoon salt*
2 *tablespoons lemon juice*
½ *teaspoon dried thyme, crumbled*
½ *teaspoon Dijon-style mustard*
½ *cup sour cream*
2 *tablespoons chopped pimiento*
1 *tablespoon minced green onion*

Sprinkle fillets with salt, lemon juice, and thyme. Place in lightly buttered 8-inch-square casserole dish. Cover tightly. Bake in a pre-heated oven at 400°F for 10 minutes.

While fish is cooking, combine mustard, sour cream, pimiento, and green onion in a small bowl. Mix well.

Remove fish from oven and brush on the sour cream–mustard mixture.

Return to oven. Cover and bake another 2 minutes. Serves 4.

Salted Codfish Supreme

Vidalena Husamudeen, Fort Bragg, North Carolina

  1 *pound salted codfish*
1½ *cups uncooked rice*
  3 *tablespoons vegetable oil*
  1 *large onion, chopped*
  1 *medium green pepper, chopped*
  3 *cloves garlic, minced*
  2 *green onions, diced*
 ½ *pound bean sprouts, rinsed*
  1 *10-ounce package pea pods, cooked and drained according to package directions*
  3 *eggs, beaten*
    soy sauce to taste

In a saucepan with 2½ cups water, boil codfish for 10 minutes, change water and boil again, until majority of salt is out. Shred fish and set aside.

Cook rice and set aside.

In a large skillet, heat oil and stir-fry onion, green pepper, garlic, and green onions until tender. Add cooked rice, bean sprouts, snow peas, eggs, fish, and soy sauce. Heat thoroughly, stirring constantly. Serves 6.

Sandi's Favorite Fish

Sandi Koetter, NAS Miramar, San Diego, California

2 *pounds freshwater bass fillets or other fish*
1 *stick butter or margarine*
1 *medium onion, diced*
2 *4-ounce cans mushrooms, drained*
¼ *cup dry white wine*
  dash lemon juice

Place fish in a 6 x 10 x 1½-inch ungreased baking dish. Bake, uncovered, in a preheated oven at 350°F for 5 minutes.

While fish is baking, melt the butter or margarine in a small saucepan. Add remaining ingredients and cook over medium heat until onion is tender.

Pour mixture over fish and bake an additional 7 minutes. Serves 6.

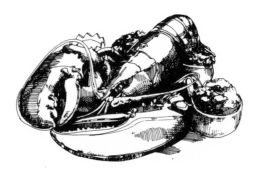

Scallop Remoulade

Mrs. Gertrud Edenfield, Robins AFB, Georgia

½ cup mayonnaise
1 tablespoon chopped green onion
1 tablespoon chopped fresh parsley
1 tablespoon dry mustard
2 teaspoons creamed horseradish
2 teaspoons vinegar
½ teaspoon paprika
¼ teaspoon Worcestershire sauce
¼ teaspoon Tabasco sauce
1 pint bay scallops, cooked
lettuce leaves

Combine all ingredients except scallops and lettuce in a medium bowl. Mix well.

Add scallops. Stir. Cover and refrigerate for at least 4 hours. Serve on lettuce leaves. Serves 3.

Seafood Crepes

Susan C. Harrison, Naval Communication Unit, Cutler, Maine

Crepe Batter
    2 cups all-purpose flour
    ½ teaspoon baking powder
    ½ teaspoon salt
 2½ cups milk
    2 eggs
    2 tablespoons butter or margarine, melted

Seafood Mixture
    3 tablespoons finely chopped scallions
    5 tablespoons butter
    ¼ cup flour
    1 cup chicken broth
    ½ cup light cream
    3 tablespoons dry sherry
    2 cups assorted fish or seafood such as scallops, shrimp, crab
       dash Tabasco sauce
       dash salt
    ½ cup whipping cream
    ¼ teaspoon nutmeg

In a medium bowl, mix flour, baking powder, and salt. Stir in remaining ingredients. Beat with hand beater until smooth.

Lightly butter a 7- or 8-inch skillet. Heat over medium heat until bubbly.

For each crepe, pour scant ¼ cup of batter into skillet. Rotate pan until thin film of batter covers bottom. Cook until light brown. Run wide spatula around edge to loosen. Turn and cook on other side until light brown. Repeat process until all batter is gone. Stack crepes, placing waxed paper between each. Refrigerate until needed.

To make filling, sauté scallions in butter in a medium saucepan for 2 minutes over medium-high heat. Sprinkle in the flour and stir well. Reduce heat. Cook for 2 minutes.

Slowly add chicken broth. Stir until mixture thickens and becomes smooth. Add cream and sherry. Cook, stirring constantly until sauce is thick, about 5 minutes.

Add shellfish and mix well. Season with Tabasco and salt. Remove from heat.

Fill each crepe with 3 tablespoons of seafood mixture. Roll crepes and place seam-side-down in a buttered 9 x 12-inch baking pan. Spoon extra filling around crepes.

Lightly whip cream and add nutmeg. Spread over crepes. Bake, uncovered, in a preheated oven at 350°F for 20–25 minutes or until sauce bubbles. Serves 4.

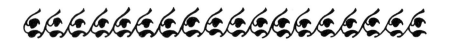

Seafood Gumbo

Nonie Schoelles, Apalachicola, Florida

3 tablespoons vegetable oil
1 medium onion, chopped
1 clove garlic, minced
1 medium green pepper, chopped
1 28-ounce can whole tomatoes, crushed
1 bay leaf
½ teaspoon salt
½ teaspoon oregano
½ teaspoon thyme
½ teaspoon pepper
  cayenne pepper to taste
1 pound seafood, such as crab meat, small shrimp, fish cut in bite-size chunks, clams, crayfish
1 10-ounce package frozen okra

In a large saucepan, heat the oil and add the onion, garlic, and green pepper. Cook over medium-high heat until wilted.

Add the tomatoes and spices. Simmer, covered, for 1 hour. Stir occasionally.

Add the seafood and okra. Cook, covered, for 30 minutes, stirring occasionally. Serve over rice. Serves 6.

Siciliano Clam Sauce
Gail Guild, Vance AFB, Oklahoma

3 tablespoons vegetable oil
½ cup chopped onion
2 cloves garlic, minced
⅔ cup chicken broth
⅓ cup dry white wine
3 tablespoons butter
¼ teaspoon dried oregano
1 6½-ounce can minced clams, undrained
½ pound linguine
⅓ cup grated Parmesan cheese
½ lemon, sliced thin
   snipped parsley for garnish

Heat the oil in a medium saucepan. Add the onion and garlic, and sauté until tender. Add chicken broth, wine, butter, and oregano. Simmer for 20 minutes.

Drain clams, reserving ¼ cup clam juice. Add clams and reserved juice, and heat thoroughly.

Meanwhile, cook linguine according to package directions. Pour clam sauce over. Sprinkle with Parmesan cheese. Garnish with lemon slices and parsley. Serves 2.

Swordfish Tropicana
Dixie L. Anderson, Mount Holly, New Jersey

1 *pound butter or margarine*
2 *tablespoons orange liqueur*
1 *6-ounce can frozen orange juice*
8 *swordfish steaks, 6–8 ounces each*
2 *bananas*

In a medium saucepan, melt the butter and clarify by skimming off the foam. Allow it to cool completely.

Add the orange liqueur and orange juice, and whisk to blend.

Broil the swordfish until it flakes easily with a fork, about 5 minutes on each side.

Spoon sauce over hot swordfish and slice banana over each portion. Serves 8.

Other Entrees

Braendende Kaelighted

Ann Marie Smith, St. Marys, Georgia

The name of this recipe means "burning love" in Danish. In order to dispel the gloom of January, Danes prefer to stay indoors and combat the weather in the company of good friends with the help of this hearty dish.

> 2 *pounds potatoes, peeled and cut into chunks*
> 8–10 *thick slices bacon, chopped*
> 3 *onions, chopped*
> ½ *stick butter*
> ½ *pint cream*
> ¼ *teaspoon pepper*
>   *nutmeg to taste*

Cook the potatoes in unsalted water until tender. Meanwhile, fry bacon with onions until onions are tender.

Drain potatoes and mash. Whip in butter gradually and then the cream. Season with spices.

Mound potatoes on platter and make a well in the center. Place bacon and onion mixture in the center. Serves 4.

Chile Relleno Casserole
Isela Henderson, Fort Belvoir, Virginia

1 *pound Monterey Jack cheese, shredded*
1 *pound cheddar cheese, shredded*
2 *4-ounce cans chopped green chilies, drained*
1 *medium onion, grated*
8 *eggs, separated*
⅔ *cup evaporated milk*
1 *tablespoon all-purpose flour*
½ *teaspoon salt*
⅛ *teaspoon pepper*
2 *tomatoes, sliced*

In a large bowl, combine the cheeses, chilies, and onion. Set aside.

With an electric mixer at high speed, beat the egg whites in a medium bowl until they form stiff peaks. Set aside.

In a small bowl, combine egg yolks, milk, flour, salt, and pepper, using an electric mixer. Gently fold this mixture into the egg whites. Fold half the egg mixture into the cheese mixture. Spoon this into a buttered, 9-inch-square casserole. Spread remaining egg mixture on top.

Bake, uncovered, in a preheated oven at 325°F for 30 minutes. Arrange tomato slices on top of casserole and bake another 15–20 minutes or until firm. Let stand 10 minutes before serving. Serves 8.

Chive and Onion Potato Bake

Wendy Ann Loftin, NAS Kingsville, Texas

1 5.5-ounce box dehydrated hash brown potatoes with onions
4 large eggs
1 8-ounce package cream cheese with chives, softened
½ cup milk
½ teaspoon pepper
⅓ cup grated Parmesan cheese

Rehydrate potatoes according to package directions. Drain well.

In a large bowl, beat eggs, cream cheese, and milk until well blended. Add potatoes, pepper, and cheese. Pour into a lightly greased 9 x 13-inch baking dish.

Bake, uncovered, in a preheated oven at 350°F for 35 minutes or until lightly browned. Let stand 5 minutes before serving. Serves 4.

Danielle's Pizza

Danielle Jones, Panama Canal Zone

Even meat eaters will enjoy this vegetarian dish.

⅔ *cup milk*
⅓ *cup vegetable oil*
2 *cups self-rising flour*
1 *24-ounce jar spaghetti sauce*
1 *tomato, sliced*
2 *small green peppers, chopped*
  other toppings as desired, such as sliced black olives, chopped green chilies, sliced mushrooms
⅓ *cup shredded cheddar cheese*
⅔ *cup shredded mozzarella cheese*
⅓ *cup grated Parmesan cheese*

In a small bowl, thoroughly mix milk and oil together.

Put the flour in a medium bowl and make a hole in the middle of the flour. Pour in the liquid. Mix with a fork until liquid is just incorporated. Do not overmix.

Pat the dough into a floured, 8 x 12 x 2-inch baking pan. Press the dough down evenly to cover the pan entirely.

Cover dough with spaghetti sauce up to ½ inch from sides of pan. Add the tomato slices, green pepper, and other toppings. Cover with cheeses.

Bake, uncovered, in preheated oven at 375°F for 17 minutes. Serves 3.

Green Chilies and Cheese Casserole
Doris Blind, NSB Bangor, Washington

1 8-ounce can whole green chilies
2 cups shredded cheddar cheese
2 cups shredded Monterey Jack cheese
3 tablespoons flour
1 13-ounce can evaporated milk
3 eggs
1 16-ounce can tomato sauce
1 4-ounce can chopped green chilies

Cut whole chilies in half lengthwise. Remove seeds and stringy parts. Place one layer of chilies in a 9 x 13-inch greased casserole dish.

Sprinkle on a layer of cheese, using a combination of cheddar and Jack. Add another layer of chilies and then cheese. Continue until casserole is filled to within 2 inches of top.

Mix flour, milk, and eggs in a small bowl. Pour over chili-cheese mixture. Bake, uncovered, in a preheated 325°F oven for 45 minutes.

Combine tomato sauce and chopped chilies in a small bowl. Pour tomato sauce on top and bake for an additional 15 minutes. Serves 6.

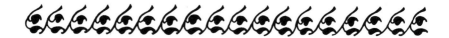

Ham Pepper Cups
Joan Sproules, Jacksonville, Florida

8 *large green peppers*
4½ *cups ground cooked ham*
3 *eggs, beaten*
½ *cup milk*
1 *cup bread crumbs*
2 *teaspoons dry mustard*
1 *teaspoon Worchestershire sauce*

Cut tops off each pepper, reserving tops. Remove seeds. Place peppers in a 9 x 12-inch cake pan with ½ inch of water. Cook on stove over high heat for 3 minutes. Drain well.

In a large mixing bowl, combine rest of ingredients. Fill peppers with ham mixture.

Stand peppers up in a 9 x 13-inch baking dish. Put tops back on. Pour ½ inch of hot water into pan. Bake, uncovered, in a preheated oven at 350°F for 45 minutes. Serves 8.

Hash Brown Pizza
Joy Evilsizor, RAF Lakenheath, England

1 *pound bulk pork sausage*
1 *8-ounce package refrigerator crescent dinner rolls*
1 *cup frozen hash brown potatoes, thawed*
1 *cup shredded cheddar cheese*
5 *eggs*
¼ *cup milk*
½ *teaspoon salt*
⅛ *teaspoon pepper*
2 *tablespoons grated Parmesan cheese*

In a large skillet, brown sausage. Drain.

Separate crescent dough into 8 triangles. Place triangles in an ungreased 12-inch pizza pan, with the points facing toward the center. Press dough over bottom and up sides of pan to form a crust.

Spoon sausage over crust. Sprinkle with potatoes. Top with cheddar cheese.

In a small bowl, beat together eggs, milk, salt, and pepper. Pour over sausage and cheese. Sprinkle Parmesan cheese over top.

Bake, uncovered, in a preheated oven at 375°F for 25–30 minutes or until eggs are set and top is lightly browned. Serves 6.

Huevos Rancheros
Doris Curls, Fort McClellan, Alabama

Try serving this over garlic toast. On each piece of toast put a slice of baked ham, then the egg and sauce.

   3 *tablespoons olive oil*
   1 *cup chopped onion*
   1 *cup chopped green pepper*
   2 *cloves garlic, minced*
   1 *tablespoon all-purpose flour*
   2 *16-ounce cans whole tomatoes, drained well and chopped*
  ½ *teaspoon dried oregano*
  ½ *teaspoon ground cumin*
   1 *teaspoon chili powder*
  ¼ *teaspoon salt*
  ¼ *teaspoon pepper*
  ¼ *cup white wine*
   6 *eggs*
  ½ *cup shredded sharp cheddar cheese*
  ¼ *cup sliced ripe olives*

Heat oil in medium saucepan. Sauté onion, green pepper, and garlic in oil until tender. Stir in flour and cook 1 minute over medium heat. Add next 7 ingredients and cook over medium heat for 5 minutes.

Pour sauce into an 8 x 12 x 2-inch casserole dish. Make 6 indentations in the sauce and break an egg into each. Sprinkle with cheese and olives.

Bake, uncovered, in a preheated oven at 350°F for 18 minutes or until eggs are set. Serve immediately. Serves 6.

Italian Sausage Casserole
Marie Marchesini, Hanscom AFB, Massachusetts

6 *mild or hot Italian sausages (about 1 pound)*
2 *tablespoons vegetable oil*
2 *cloves garlic, minced*
¼ *pound mushrooms, sliced thin*
2 *green peppers, cut into 1-inch squares*
2 *large potatoes, cut into bite-size pieces*
1 *teaspoon oregano*
1 *teaspoon basil*
1 *teaspoon salt*
1 *1-pound, 12-ounce can whole tomatoes, crushed*
¼ *cup dry white wine*
1 *17-ounce can peas (optional)*

Cut sausages into thirds. In a large skillet, heat oil and brown the sausage. Remove from skillet and set aside.

Add garlic, mushrooms, peppers, and potatoes to the skillet and sauté 5 minutes. Add seasonings, tomatoes, and wine. Stir.

Return sausage to skillet. Simmer, uncovered, for 45 minutes on low heat, stirring occasionally. If using peas, add for last 5 minutes. Serves 4.

Jalapeno-Corn Quiche
Mrs. Doris Curls, Fort McClellan, Alabama

This recipe also makes nice hors d'oeuvres if you use miniature muffin tins instead of the regular pie tin.

    1 *unbaked 9-inch pastry crust*
    3 *slices uncooked bacon*
    ½ *cup chopped onion*
    1 *17-ounce can creamed corn, undrained*
1 or 2 *jalapeno peppers, seeded and minced*
    2 *eggs, beaten*
    ½ *cup half-and-half*
    ½ *cup shredded cheddar cheese*
    1 *tablespoon all-purpose flour*
    ¼ *teaspoon salt*
    ⅛ *teaspoon pepper*
    additional jalapeno slices for garnish (optional)

Prick bottom and sides of crust with a fork. Bake in preheated oven at 400°F for 3 minutes. Remove from oven, gently prick with fork again, and return to oven for 5 more minutes. Cool on rack.

Cook bacon in a skillet until crisp. Remove bacon and reserve 1 tablespoon bacon grease in skillet. Crumble bacon and set aside.

Sauté onion in bacon drippings until tender. Drain well.

In a large bowl, combine onion, corn, peppers, eggs, half-and-half, cheese, flour, salt, and pepper. Mix well.

Pour into pastry shell. Sprinkle bacon on top. Bake in a preheated oven at 375°F for 45 minutes or until set. Garnish with additional jalapeno slices if desired. Serves 6.

Knife and Fork Stew

Evelyn E. Gunn, Randolph AFB, Texas

¾ pound kielbasa, cut into small pieces
1 cup chopped celery
1 cup chopped carrots
1 28-ounce can stewed tomatoes
½ envelope dry onion soup mix
1 tablespoon granulated sugar
  Tabasco sauce to taste
½ 5-ounce package frozen green beans
½ 5-ounce package frozen whole kernel corn
½ 16-ounce package frozen hash browns
½ 5-ounce package frozen green peas

In a large kettle, combine kielbasa, celery, carrots, tomatoes, onion soup mix, sugar, and Tabasco sauce. Simmer, covered, over medium heat for 20–30 minutes.

Add green beans, corn, and hash browns. Cook, covered, on low heat for 10 minutes.

Add peas and cook gently, covered, for 5 to 10 minutes. Serves 4.

Macaroni and Cheese Special
Elsie Faye Alley, Sparta, North Carolina

1½ cups grated cheddar cheese
1 10¾-ounce can condensed cream of chicken soup
1 medium onion, minced
½ green pepper, minced
2 tablespoons mayonnaise
1 cup evaporated milk
¾ stick butter or margarine, melted
2 cups cooked macaroni
   salt and pepper to taste

In a large bowl, combine all ingredients in order given, stirring well after each addition.

Turn into a greased 9-inch round casserole dish. Bake, covered, in a preheated oven at 350°F for 30 minutes or until bubbly. Serves 4.

Macaroni Mousse

Chris Cummings, Luke AFB, Arizona

1 *cup cooked macaroni, diced*
1 *cup milk, scalded*
1 *cup cubed American or cheddar cheese*
1 *cup bread crumbs*
¼ *cup butter or margarine, melted*
1 *pimiento, chopped*
1 *teaspoon chopped parsley*
1 *tablespoon chopped onion*
   dash salt
   dash cayenne
3 *eggs, well beaten*

Combine macaroni, milk, cheese, bread crumbs, and butter in a large bowl.

Mix in pimiento, parsley, onion, salt, and cayenne. Stir in eggs.

Pour mixture into a greased 8-inch casserole dish. Bake, covered, in preheated oven at 325°F for 45 minutes. Serves 4.

Meatless Loaf

Mrs. Nancy Knott, Long Beach, California

2 cups cooked brown rice
1½ cups grated cheddar cheese
1 cup grated carrot
½ cup plain yogurt
4 eggs, beaten
¼ onion, chopped fine
¼ green pepper, chopped fine
½ cup finely chopped mushrooms
½ teaspoon dried basil
2 tablespoons chopped fresh parsley
¼ cup chopped black olives

Combine all ingredients in a large bowl. Mix well.

Place in a greased 4 x 8-inch loaf pan. Place loaf pan in a larger roasting pan filled with hot water to within 1 inch of the top of loaf pan.

Bake, uncovered, in a preheated oven at 350°F for 1 hour or until a knife inserted in the center comes out clean. Serve with cheese sauce, if desired. Serves 4.

Northern Michigan Pie

Bonnie L. Baldwin, Virginia Beach, Virginia

1 small red cabbage, chopped
1 large onion, chopped
3 carrots, diced
6 potatoes, diced very small
1 small rutabaga, diced
½ teaspoon salt
¼ teaspoon pepper
⅓ stick butter
    pie crust for top and bottom of pie

Combine all ingredients except crust in a large bowl. Mix well.

Line a 9-inch cake pan with ½ of crust. Turn vegetable mixture into pan. Top with remaining crust. Make several slits in top.

Bake in a preheated oven at 325°F for 1 hour. Serves 6.

Sausage Rigatoni

Carol Barclay, Portland, Texas

2 *cups uncooked rigatoni noodles*
1 *pound ground sausage, mild or hot*
  basil to taste
  oregano to taste
  garlic powder to taste
  salt and pepper to taste
1 *quart tomato sauce*
½ *pound provolone cheese, grated*
1 *cup sour cream*
½ *pound mozzarella cheese, grated*
½ *cup grated Parmesan cheese*

Boil noodles in salted water until tender. Drain.

Sauté sausage with spices until brown. Drain.

Butter a 9-inch-square casserole and layer as follows: rigatoni, half the tomato sauce, provolone, sour cream, sausage, mozzarella, and remaining tomato sauce. Top with Parmesan cheese.

Bake, uncovered, in a preheated oven at 350°F for 30 minutes. May be made ahead and frozen. Serves 6.

Spinach Quiche

Mrs. John (Marian) Ramey, Fayetteville, Georgia

Spinach Quiche reheats beautifully; add 4–6 slices of cooked and crumbled bacon for a different flavor.

    1   9-inch ready-to-bake pie crust
  2–3   tablespoons prepared mustard
    6   ounces Swiss cheese, grated, divided
    1   bunch green onions, white part only
    3   tablespoons butter or margarine
    1   cup cottage cheese
    3   eggs
    1   10-ounce package frozen chopped spinach, cooked only till
        separated, then drained
        salt and pepper to taste
   ¼   teaspoon nutmeg
   ½   cup milk
        dash Tabasco sauce

Brush pie crust with mustard. Spread 2 ounces of cheese on top of the mustard. Bake in a preheated oven at 350°F for 10 minutes. Remove from oven and set aside.

Chop the whites of the green onion and sauté in butter or margarine until tender, about 5 minutes.

In a food processor or blender, puree cottage cheese until smooth. Add eggs and blend. Add remaining ingredients along with sautéed onions, and blend well.

Pour into crust and bake, uncovered, at 350°F for 25–30 minutes or until set. Serves 6.

Spinach-Rice Casserole

Patricia Marie Bisgaard, Hanford, California

1 10-ounce package frozen chopped spinach, cooked according to
   package directions and drained well
3 cups cooked brown rice
½ cup melted butter or margarine
4 eggs, beaten
1 pound sharp cheddar cheese, shredded
1 cup nonfat milk
1 tablespoon chopped onion
1½ tablespoons soy sauce
½ teaspoon salt
¼ teaspoon thyme
¼ teaspoon marjoram
¼ teaspoon rosemary

In a large bowl, combine all ingredients. Mix well.

Pour into a 10 x 13-inch greased casserole dish. Bake in a pre-heated oven at 350°F for 1 hour or until set. Serves 6.

Vegetable Enchiladas
Mrs. Bonnie Bakken, Mather AFB, California

Enchilada Sauce
¼ cup vegetable oil
1 medium onion, chopped
1 clove garlic, minced
1 sprig parsley
1 6-ounce can tomato paste
1 tablespoon vinegar
1 tablespoon sugar
1 tablespoon chili powder
⅛ teaspoon cayenne
½ teaspoon salt
½ teaspoon dried oregano
½ teaspoon cumin seed

Filling
1 small onion, chopped
8 medium mushrooms, sliced
2 tablespoons vegetable oil
1 medium zucchini, finely chopped
2 handfuls mung bean sprouts
1 cup finely chopped broccoli
12 large flour tortillas
1–2 cups grated cheddar cheese

To make sauce, heat oil in small saucepan. Add onion and garlic and sauté till tender. Add parsley, tomato paste, and ½ cup water. Simmer 3 minutes, uncovered. Add 1 cup water, vinegar, sugar, and seasonings. Simmer 15 minutes, covered.

To make filling, sauté onion and mushrooms in oil over low heat in a large skillet. Stir in zucchini, bean sprouts, and broccoli. Add about ¼ to ½ cup of sauce to moisten. Stir well.

Heat tortillas in oven or on griddle. Place ¼ cup vegetable mixture in middle of tortilla. Add small handful of cheese. Roll.

Place seam-side down in a 9 x 13-inch ungreased baking dish. Top with sauce and more cheese. Cover with foil. Bake in a preheated oven at 350°F for 15 minutes or until cheese is bubbly. Serves 6.

Located in the heart of Fort Lee, Virginia, Mifflin Hall is the headquarters building for the U.S. Army Quartermaster Center and School. The statue superimposed in front of the building is of Robert E. Lee, the general for whom the post is named. This famous work is located in nearby Richmond. *Drawing by Ken Crawford, courtesy of Fort Lee.*

Side Dishes

Around the World Potato Casserole
Mildred Jackson Burress, Florala, Alabama

1 2-pound bag frozen hash browns, thawed
1 10¾-ounce can condensed cream of chicken soup
1 cup sour cream
¼ teaspoon pepper
1 teaspoon salt
2 cups shredded cheddar cheese
¾ cup melted butter or margarine, divided
2 cups crushed corn flakes

Combine potatoes, soup, sour cream, pepper, salt, cheese, and
½ cup melted butter or margarine in a large bowl. Mix well. Turn into
a greased 9-inch-square casserole dish.

Combine the remaining butter or margarine with the corn flakes
in a small bowl. Cover potatoes with corn flake mixture.

Bake, uncovered, in a preheated oven at 350°F for 45 minutes.
Serves 6.

Betty's Squash Parmesan

Betty Compton Simmons, Lindsey Air Force Station,
Wiesbaden, Germany

6 *medium summer squash*
2 *medium onions, chopped*
1 *green pepper, chopped*
1 *cup mayonnaise*
1¼ *cup grated Parmesan cheese, divided*
2 *large eggs*

Wash and slice squash into ¼-inch pieces. Steam with onions and green pepper until tender.

In separate bowl, mix mayonnaise, 1 cup cheese, and eggs. Add squash and combine well.

Turn into an ungreased 8-inch-square casserole dish. Bake, uncovered, in a preheated oven at 350°F for 35–45 minutes.

Sprinkle remaining ¼ cup cheese on top just before serving. Serves 8.

Broccoli with Wine Sauce

Mrs. Ruth Newberry, Robins AFB, Georgia

   1 *bunch (about 2 pounds) broccoli, washed and cut into stalks*
  ½ *cup mayonnaise*
  ½ *teaspoon lemon juice*
  ⅛ *teaspoon curry powder*
⅛–¼ *cup white wine*

Steam broccoli until tender.

In a small saucepan, combine mayonnaise, lemon juice, curry, and enough white wine to make a thin sauce. Heat but do not boil.

Drizzle sauce over broccoli and serve. Serves 4.

Cheese Scalloped Carrots
Julie Poe, McClellan AFB, California

6 medium carrots, sliced thin
2 tablespoons butter or margarine
½ onion, minced
2 tablespoons flour
½ teaspoon salt
   dash pepper
⅛ teaspoon dry mustard
⅛ teaspoon celery salt
¼ teaspoon garlic powder
1 cup milk
¼ pound American cheese, sliced thin
¼ cup bread crumbs

Cook carrots, covered, in 1 inch of boiling water until tender, about 5 minutes. Drain.

In a small saucepan, melt butter or margarine and sauté onion for 3 minutes over medium-high heat. Stir in flour and spices, then milk. Cook, stirring with whisk, until sauce is smooth and thick.

Arrange a layer of carrots on the bottom of an ungreased 5 x 9-inch baking dish. Place some cheese on top. Repeat until carrots and cheese are gone, ending with a layer of carrots. Pour sauce over all. Top with bread crumbs.

Bake, uncovered, in a preheated oven at 350°F for 35–40 minutes or until heated through. Serves 4.

Cowboy Potatoes

Romona R. DeWolf, Fort Lee, Virginia

8 medium potatoes
½ cup chopped celery
1 tablespoon chopped onion
1 teaspoon salt
⅛ teaspoon pepper
¼ cup butter

Wash potatoes well, but do not peel. Slice very thin into an 8-inch-square casserole dish.

Fold in chopped celery and onion, salt, and pepper. Dot with butter.

Bake, covered, in a preheated oven at 350°F for 45 minutes or until tender. Serves 6.

Danish Cabbage

Melissa Nelson, Hunter Army Air Field, Georgia

1 *large head green cabbage, chopped*
1 *cup sour cream*
1 *teaspoon caraway seed*
½ *teaspoon salt*
½ *teaspoon white pepper*

Bring 3 cups water to a boil in a medium saucepan. Add the cabbage and boil, covered, for 6–8 minutes on medium-high heat. Drain.

In the top of a double boiler, toss cabbage with remaining ingredients. Cover and cook gently for 15 minutes. Serves 6.

Garden Eggplant Casserole
James D. Phillips, Eglin AFB, Florida

1 *medium eggplant, peeled and diced into ½-inch cubes*
1 *teaspoon granulated sugar*
2 *cups water*
1 *10¾-ounce can condensed cream of mushroom soup*
1 *4-ounce can chopped mushrooms, undrained*
¼ *cup diced onion*
1 *cup shredded American or cheddar cheese*
20 *saltine crackers, crushed*
2 *eggs, beaten*
1½ *tablespoons butter or margarine, melted*

In a medium saucepan, bring eggplant, sugar, and water to a boil. Boil for 5 minutes. Drain very well.

Combine all ingredients in a large bowl and mix well. Turn into a greased 8-inch-square casserole dish. Bake, uncovered, in a preheated oven at 350°F for 1 hour. Serves 4.

Hominy-Cheese Casserole
Gail Ann Kenna, Maxwell AFB, Alabama

2 *16-ounce cans white hominy*
3 *green onions*
2 *4-ounce cans diced green chilies*
1 *clove garlic, crushed*
4 *cups grated cheddar cheese*

Drain hominy. Put onions and hominy through a food processor or food chopper.

In a small bowl, mix chilies and garlic.

In a greased, 9-inch round casserole dish, place a layer of the hominy-onion mixture, then a layer of cheese, then chili mixture. Alternate until all ingredients are gone, ending with cheese.

Bake, uncovered, in a preheated oven at 350°F for 45 minutes, or until casserole is bubbly. Serves 6.

Irene's Zucchini Bake

Irene Riordan, Las Vegas, Nevada

6 *medium zucchini, coarsely grated*
1 *green pepper, coarsely grated*
1 *medium onion, coarsely grated*
3 *eggs, well beaten*
½ *cup butter or margarine, melted*
⅓ *cup grated Parmesan cheese*
2 *cups corn bread stuffing*
⅓ *cup shredded cheddar or taco cheese*

Mix together grated zucchini, green pepper, and onion in a large bowl. Add eggs, butter or margarine, Parmesan cheese, and stuffing. Mix well.

Turn into a greased 9 x 13-inch casserole dish. Top with cheese. Bake, covered, in a preheated oven at 350°F for 40 minutes. Cut into 12 3-inch squares. Serves 6.

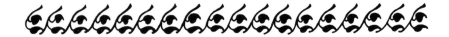

Juanita's Zucchini Casserole
Mrs. Walter J. Palmer, Santa Fe, New Mexico

2 *eggs*
½ *cup vegetable oil*
1 *cup grated Monterey Jack or Parmesan cheese*
1 *cup Bisquick*
1 *clove garlic, minced*
2 *tablespoons minced fresh parsley*
  dash pepper
4 *cups thinly sliced zucchini*
  bread crumbs to cover, about ¼ cup

Mix first 7 ingredients in a large mixing bowl. Blend thoroughly. Add zucchini and stir gently.

Butter a 7 x 11-inch baking dish and spread a thin layer of bread crumbs on the bottom. Pour zucchini batter over crumbs.

Bake, uncovered, in a preheated oven at 325°F for 35 minutes. Serves 4.

Lima Bean Casserole

Mrs. Walter J. Palmer, Santa Fe, New Mexico

  1 *10-ounce package frozen lima beans, thawed*
  4 *slices uncooked bacon, cut into ½-inch strips*
  1 *large onion, diced*
  1 *tablespoon molasses*
  2 *cups canned whole tomatoes, crushed and drained*
  1 *tablespoon brown sugar*
 ¼ *teaspoon chili powder*

Combine lima beans, bacon, and onion in a 10-inch-square casserole dish.

In a medium bowl, combine rest of ingredients and mix well. Pour into lima bean mixture and stir well.

Bake, covered, in preheated oven at 375°F for 45 minutes. Serves 6.

Onion and Corn Casserole

Gloria Chasse, West Barnstable, Massachusetts

¼ cup butter or margarine
¾ cup chopped green peppers
1 clove garlic, crushed
¼ cup all-purpose flour
⅔ cup milk
¾ teaspoon salt
¼ teaspoon pepper
½ teaspoon basil
½ teaspoon oregano
1 cup grated Parmesan cheese, divided
1 cup canned whole tomatoes, drained well
1 10-ounce can corn, drained well
1 10-ounce can whole onions, drained well

In a medium saucepan, melt butter or margarine. Add green peppers and garlic and sauté until tender. Stir in flour and blend to coat peppers. Add milk and spices. Stir until sauce thickens.

Remove from heat and stir in ½ cup Parmesan cheese. Mix well. Add tomatoes. Heat gently until mixture thickens again.

Add corn and onions and stir well. Turn into 12-inch casserole dish. Sprinkle remaining cheese on top and bake, uncovered, in preheated oven at 350°F for 50 minutes. Serves 6.

Panamanian Rice

Mrs. Claude M. Briggs, USM Ret., McLean, Virginia

4 strips bacon
1 medium onion, chopped
½ green pepper, chopped
3 stalks celery, chopped
1 cup uncooked rice
 salt and pepper to taste
1 tablespoon poultry seasoning
½ teaspoon curry powder
¼ teaspoon paprika
 dash cayenne
1 10½-ounce can beef bouillion
10½ ounces water

Fry bacon in a skillet until crisp. Crumble and set aside. Save bacon drippings.

Lightly brown onion, green pepper, celery, and rice in bacon drippings on medium-high heat until vegetables are tender. Add salt, pepper, poultry seasoning, curry, paprika, and cayenne.

Add bouillion and water. Bring to a boil and simmer, uncovered, for 3–5 minutes.

Pour mixture into a 9-inch-square casserole dish and bake, covered, in a preheated oven at 350°F for 45 minutes. Add crumbled bacon and bake, uncovered, for additional 15 minutes. Serves 6.

Potato Pierogi

Helen Dudek Perrine, Homestead, Florida

2 *cups all-purpose flour*
2 *eggs*
1 *teaspoon salt, divided*
⅓ *cup water*
5 *tablespoons butter or margarine, divided*
½ *cup chopped onion*
¼ *teaspoon white pepper*
2 *cups cold mashed potatoes*
   sour cream (optional)

Combine flour, eggs, ½ teaspoon salt, and water in a mixing bowl. Mix well to make a medium-soft dough. Knead well until dough is firm. Cover with a warm towel and let rest 10 minutes.

Meanwhile, melt 2 tablespoons butter or margarine in a small saucepan. Sauté onion for 5 minutes, or until tender. Add pepper and remaining salt. Remove from heat and mix in potatoes.

Divide dough in half. On a floured surface, roll out each half to about ⅛ inch thick. Using a round cookie cutter or the rim of a drinking glass, cut out circles about 3 inches in diameter.

Place about 1 teaspoon onion-potato mixture in the center of each circle. Fold in half and press firmly to seal.

Drop into boiling water and cook gently for 5 minutes or until pierogi float to the top. Remove with a slotted spoon.

Melt remaining butter in skillet. Fry pierogi on medium-high heat until golden brown, about 5 minutes. Serve with sour cream, if desired. Serves 4.

Rice Consommé
Lynn J. Catalina, Kirkland AFB, New Mexico

1 *medium onion, sliced thin*
1 *stick butter or margarine*
1 *cup uncooked rice*
1 *4-ounce can mushrooms, drained*
2 *10-ounce cans chicken or beef consommé*
½ *teaspoon salt*
½ *teaspoon pepper*
½ *teaspoon garlic powder*

In a medium saucepan, sauté onion in butter or margarine until tender.

Transfer onion to a 9-inch casserole dish. Add remaining ingredients and combine well. Bake, covered, in a preheated oven at 350°F for one hour or until all liquid is absorbed. Serves 6.

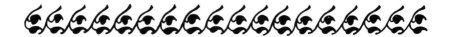

Soy Garlic Mushrooms

Yolanda Nieves, Stuttgart Army Base, West Germany

1 pound mushrooms, washed and sliced
½ cup water
¼ cup soy sauce
¼ cup olive oil
⅛ teaspoon garlic powder
1 clove garlic, minced

In a medium saucepan, cook mushrooms in water for 5 minutes. Drain.

Return mushrooms to pan. Add soy sauce, oil, and garlic. Cook for 5 minutes. Serve with a slotted spoon if using for a side dish. Serve with liquid if using as a topping for meat. Serves 4.

Special Carrots
Gail A. Guild, Vance AFB, Oklahoma

  1 *pound carrots, scraped and sliced diagonally in ½-inch slices*
  ½ *cup chopped celery*
  ¼ *cup chopped onion*
  ¼ *cup dry white wine*
  2 *tablespoons butter or margarine*
  2 *tablespoons granulated sugar*
  ¼ *teaspoon dried dill*

Combine all ingredients in a medium saucepan. Bring to a boil.
Cover, reduce heat and simmer 10–12 minutes. Serves 6.

Unique Cabbage Casserole
Sylvia R. Myers, York, Maine

1 *medium head green cabbage, cut into 2-inch wedges*
¼ *cup butter or margarine*
¼ *cup all-purpose flour*
½ *teaspoon salt*
¼ *teaspoon pepper*
2 *cups milk*
½ *green pepper, chopped*
½ *onion, chopped*
⅔ *cup shredded cheddar cheese*
½ *cup mayonnaise*
3 *tablespoons chili sauce*

Boil the cabbage in a large saucepan in 2 inches of salted water until tender, about 15 minutes. Drain. Place cabbage in the bottom of an ungreased 9 x 13-inch casserole dish. Set aside.

Combine butter and flour in saucepan over low heat. Stir until smooth and bubbly. Add salt, pepper, and milk. Whisk constantly over medium heat until sauce is smooth and thick.

Pour sauce over cabbage and bake uncovered in a preheated oven at 375°F for 20 minutes. Remove from oven.

Combine remaining ingredients in a small bowl. Mix well. Spread over top of cabbage. Return to oven and bake at 400°F for an additional 20 minutes. Serves 8.

Breads and Rolls

Apple-Walnut Muffins

Wendy Ann Loftin, NAS Kingsville, Texas

¾ cup milk
2 eggs
¼ cup butter or margarine, melted
2 cups unbleached flour
¾ cup granulated sugar, divided
1 tablespoon baking powder
1½ teaspoons cinnamon, divided
1½ cups coarsely grated apples
½ cup chopped walnuts

In a large bowl, whisk together milk, eggs, and melted butter until well blended.

Combine flour, ½ cup sugar, baking powder, and 1 teaspoon cinnamon. Blend into milk mixture until just moistened. Stir in apples. Spoon into greased muffin tins.

Mix nuts with remaining ¼ cup sugar and ½ teaspoon cinnamon. Sprinkle an even amount on top of each muffin.

Bake in a preheated oven at 375°F for 15 minutes or until a toothpick inserted in the center comes out clean. Cool 10 minutes in pan, then invert onto rack. Makes 1 dozen.

Best Pumpkin Bread
Betty Malhiot, Fairfield, California

6 *eggs*
1½ *cups Crisco*
3½ *cups sugar*
1 *cup water*
2 *cups pureed pumpkin*
5¼ *cups flour*
2¼ *teaspoons salt*
1 *tablespoon baking soda*
2½ *teaspoons cinnamon*
2½ *teaspoons nutmeg*
2 *cups chopped walnuts and/or pecans*

In a large bowl, combine all ingredients except nuts. Beat by hand until well blended, about 3 minutes. Mix in nuts.

Pour into 2 greased loaf pans. Bake in a preheated oven at 350°F for 1½ hours or until a toothpick inserted in the center comes out clean. Makes 2 large loaves.

Butter Dips

Debbie Howard, Dyess AFB, Texas

2¼ cups all-purpose flour
1 tablespoon granulated sugar
3½ teaspoons baking powder
1½ teaspoons salt
1 cup milk
⅓ cup butter or margarine, melted

Sift dry ingredients together in a large bowl. Add milk and stir slowly until dough becomes sticky.

On a lightly floured surface, roll dough into an 8 x 12-inch rectangle. Cut in half lengthwise. Cut each half into 16 strips. Dip each strip into melted butter and place on an ungreased 9 x 13-inch cake pan.

Bake in a preheated oven at 450°F for 10–15 minutes, or until lightly brown. Serves 6.

Buttermilk Honey Bread

Joy Marie Watkins, NSB, Bangor, Washington

   1 *envelope dry yeast*
 ¾ *cup warm water*
   3 *tablespoons plus 1 teaspoon honey, divided*
   6 *cups sifted, unbleached, all-purpose flour (approximately)*
1½ *cups lukewarm buttermilk*
 ¼ *stick unsalted butter, melted and cooled*
   1 *tablespoon salt*

Sprinkle dry yeast over warm water (105°F to 115°F) in small bowl. Add 1 teaspoon honey and stir to dissolve. Let stand until foamy, about 10 minutes.

In a large bowl, combine 2 cups flour, remaining honey, buttermilk, butter, and salt. Add yeast mixture and whisk until smooth, about 3 minutes.

Mix in remaining flour, ½ cup at a time, until dough is too stiff to stir. Knead on a lightly floured surface until smooth and satiny, about 10 minutes, kneading in more flour if dough is sticky.

Grease a large ceramic or glass bowl. Add dough, turning to oil entire surface. Cover bowl with a wet towel. Let rise in a warm place until doubled, about 1½ hours.

Gently knead dough until deflated. Cut in half. Knead each half into a round. Pull two opposite sides under to form oval. Place on greased cookie sheet, seam side down. Cover with wet towel and let rise in warm place until doubled, about 45 minutes.

Bake in the center of a preheated oven at 375°F for 45 minutes or until loaves sound hollow when tapped. Immediately transfer to cooling racks. Cool completely before serving. Makes 2 loaves.

David's Hamburger Buns
Dixie L. Anderson, Mount Holly, New Jersey

> 2 cakes yeast
> 2 cups warm water
> 2 cups warm milk
> 1½ teaspoons salt
> ¾ cup granulated sugar
> ½ cup lard or margarine
> 10 cups all-purpose flour (approximately)

Mix yeast and water in a large bowl. Add all other ingredients except flour and mix well.

Add 8 cups of flour. Blend well. Let stand 10 minutes. Add approximately 2 more cups of flour and knead until dough is elastic. Cover and let rise in a warm place for 1 hour.

Punch down dough and shape into balls the size of a tennis ball.

Place on an ungreased cookie sheet and flatten into hamburger bun shape. Cover and let rise in a warm place until doubled in size, about 2–3 hours.

Bake in a preheated oven at 350°F for 15 minutes or until golden brown. Makes 2½ dozen.

173

Easy Homemade Rolls
Anita Seaman, Bolling AFB, Washington, D.C.

 2 1-pound loaves frozen bread dough
½ cup butter or margarine, melted
 1 cup firmly packed light brown sugar
 1 6-ounce package vanilla pudding (not instant)
 2 tablespoons milk
1½ teaspoons cinnamon
 1 3-ounce package pecan pieces (optional)

Thaw loaves (about 2 hours) but do not allow to rise. Break up 1 loaf into small pieces and place in the bottom of a greased 9 x 13-inch pan.

In a large bowl, combine melted butter, brown sugar, pudding mix, milk, and cinnamon. Add nuts if desired. Stir well and pour over broken loaf.

Break second loaf in same manner and place over first. Cover and let rise at room temperature for about 2½ hours.

Bake, uncovered, in a preheated oven at 350°F for 30 minutes or until lightly browned. While still warm, invert onto serving dish so brown sugar mixture runs over rolls. Serves 10.

Grandma Parker's Orange Bread

Kathleen Parker O'Beirne, Arlington, Virginia

> *peel from 2 oranges*
> 1 *teaspoon salt, divided*
> 1 *cup granulated sugar*
> ¾ *cup water*
> 1 *egg, beaten*
> 1 *cup milk*
> 3 *cups all-purpose flour*
> 4 *teaspoons baking powder*
> 1 *tablespoon melted butter or margarine*

In a medium saucepan, bring orange peel and ½ teaspoon salt to a boil. Cover and boil gently for 15 minutes. Drain and cut peel into ½ x ⅛-inch slices.

Return peel to saucepan. Add sugar and ¾ cup water. Boil, uncovered, for 15 minutes on medium-high heat, stirring occasionally. Remove from heat and cool for about 15 minutes.

In a large bowl, combine egg, milk, flour, baking powder, ½ teaspoon salt, and butter or margarine. Add cooled orange mixture. Stir. Dough will be very sticky.

Turn into a greased tube pan. Bake in a preheated oven at 350°F for 40 minutes or until a toothpick inserted in the center comes out clean. To serve, slice thin and spread with butter. Serves 18.

Mexican Corn Bread

Mary G. Weston, Willingbon, New Jersey

This very moist corn bread is more easily eaten with a fork.

> 1½ cups yellow cornmeal
> 1 8-ounce can creamed corn
> 1 cup sour cream
> ⅔ cup vegetable oil
> 1 4-ounce can diced green chilies
> 2 eggs
> 1½ cups grated cheddar cheese

Mix all ingredients except cheese in a large bowl. Pour half the batter into a greased 8-inch-square pan. Sprinkle half the cheese on top. Add remaining batter and then sprinkle on remaining cheese.

Bake, uncovered, in a preheated oven at 375°F for 45 minutes or until a toothpick inserted in the center comes out clean. Serves 12.

Parmesan Cheese Rolls
Vivien R. O'Rourke, Sneads Ferry, North Carolina

1 *stick butter or margarine, melted*
2 *8-ounce packages refrigerator dinner rolls*
½ *cup grated Parmesan cheese*

Drizzle one-third of the butter or margarine into a Bundt pan. Place 1 package of rolls on bottom. Sprinkle half the Parmesan cheese on top.

Drizzle half of the remaining butter over rolls. Stagger the second package of rolls on top. Sprinkle remaining cheese. Drizzle rest of butter.

Bake in a preheated oven at 350°F for 15–18 minutes, making sure the tops of rolls are very brown so that the underneath will be cooked. Serves 12.

Pikelets

Connie A. Payne, Eglin AFB, Florida

Pikelets, from an Australian recipe, are good for breakfast or for snacks.

> 2 *cups self-rising flour*
> 1 *teaspoon cream of tartar*
> 1 *tablespoon granulated sugar*
> 1 *teaspoon baking soda*
> 1 *cup milk*
> 2 *eggs, beaten*

Sift flour and cream of tartar into a large bowl. Add sugar and mix well. Make a hollow in the center of the dry ingredients. Set aside.

Blend baking soda with a little milk and then add more milk to reach 1 cup total. Combine milk and eggs. Beat well.

Pour milk mixture in the center of dry ingredients. Mix well with wooden spoon.

Heat a greased skillet. Drop mixture from a teaspoon onto skillet. When surface of batter begins to bubble, turn pikelets over and brown other side. Spread with Cool Whip and strawberry or raspberry jam, if desired. Serves 6.

RRR's Carrot Spice Muffins
Mrs. Heather A. Rahorn, Holloman AFB, New Mexico

These muffins won first prize in the 1986 Healthful Foods competition at the Dental Health Fair at Fort Bliss, Texas.

> 2 *tablespoons honey*
> 1 *egg white*
> ½ *cup plain yogurt*
> ½ *teaspoon vanilla extract*
> ½ *teaspoon molasses*
> ½ *cup water*
> 1½ *cups whole wheat flour*
> 1 *teaspoon baking soda*
> 1 *teaspoon baking powder*
> ½ *teaspoon cinnamon*
> ¼ *teaspoon nutmeg*
> ¼ *teaspoon allspice*
> ¼ *teaspoon ginger*
> 1 *cup raisins*
> ½ *cup chopped walnuts*
> 3 *medium carrots, grated*

In a large bowl, beat the first 6 ingredients with an electric mixer until smooth.

Add the flour, soda, baking powder, cinnamon, nutmeg, allspice, and ginger. Stir well by hand. Add more water if necessary to get a very moist, but not runny, batter.

Add raisins, walnuts, and carrots. Mix well.

Fill 12 greased muffin tins to within ¼ inch of the tops of the cups. Cook in a preheated oven at 400°F for 18–20 minutes or until a toothpick inserted in the center comes out clean. Makes 12.

Scottish Oat Scones

Margaret Burns, Camarillo, California

⅓ cup butter or margarine, melted
⅓ cup milk
1 egg, beaten
1½ cups all-purpose flour
¼ cup granulated sugar
1 tablespoon baking powder
¼ teaspoon salt
¼ teaspoon cream of tartar
1¼ cups quick oats
⅓ cup raisins

Combine butter or margarine, milk, and egg in a large bowl. Set aside.

Sift together flour, sugar, baking powder, salt, and cream of tartar. Add to milk mixture. Add oats and raisins and mix well.

Form the dough into a ball and pat into an 8-inch circle on a lightly floured cookie sheet or pizza pan. Cut into 8 wedges. Separate wedges slightly and bake in a preheated oven at 400°F for 12–15 minutes or until light brown. Serve warm, with applesauce if desired. Makes 8.

Strawberry Bread

Joy Watkins, Bremerton, Washington

    1 *cup chopped strawberries*
  ¾ *cup granulated sugar, divided*
    2 *cups all-purpose flour*
  ½ *teaspoon baking powder*
  ½ *teaspoon salt*
  ½ *cup butter or margarine, melted and cooled*
    2 *eggs*
1½ *cups Cool Whip, thawed*

Cream Cheese Spread
    1 *8-ounce package cream cheese, softened*
    1 *tablespoon milk*
  ½ *cup Cool Whip, thawed*

In a small bowl, combine strawberries and ¼ cup sugar. Set aside.

In a large bowl, combine remaining sugar, flour, baking powder, and salt. Add butter and eggs. Add strawberries and mix gently. Fold in Cool Whip.

Pour into a greased 5 x 9-inch loaf pan. Bake in a preheated oven at 350°F for 1 hour or until a toothpick inserted in the center comes out clean. Cool 5 minutes and then remove from pan. Cool completely.

Meanwhile, make Cream Cheese Spread by combining cream cheese and milk in a small bowl using an electric mixer. Blend well. Fold in Cool Whip. Spread on cooled bread slices. Serves 16.

Vanilla Pudding Cinnamon Rolls
Naomi J. Moore, Altus AFB, Oklahoma

2 cups milk
1 3-ounce package instant vanilla pudding
¾ cup butter or margarine, melted, divided
¼ cup granulated sugar
2 eggs
1 teaspoon salt
2 packages dry yeast
½ cup warm water
7 cups all-purpose flour (approximately)

Filling
1 cup brown sugar, firmly packed
1 cup raisins
2 teaspoons cinnamon

Frosting
3 tablespoons butter or margarine, softened
2 cups powdered sugar
½ teaspoon almond extract
2–3 tablespoons milk

In a large bowl, mix milk and pudding according to pudding package directions. Add ½ cup melted butter or margarine, sugar, eggs, and salt.

In a small bowl, dissolve yeast in warm water. Add to pudding mixture. Stir well. Gradually add 6 cups unsifted flour, mixing well. Add more flour if necessary to reach kneading consistency.

Knead on floured surface for about 5 minutes, kneading in remaining cup of flour. Place in lightly greased bowl. Cover. Let rise in a warm place until double in bulk, about 1 hour.

Make filling by combining all ingredients in a small bowl. When dough has risen, divide in two. Roll each ball out on a floured surface

into a 9 x 13-inch rectangle. Brush each with half of the remaining ¼ cup melted butter and sprinkle on half the filling.

Roll up each rectangle tightly and cut into 2-inch slices. Divide the slices equally into 2 greased 9 x 13-inch pans. Let rise until double, about 1 hour.

Bake in a preheated oven at 350°F for 30 minutes or until lightly brown. Let cool 15 minutes.

While rolls are cooling, make frosting. Combine butter or margarine, sugar, and almond extract. Add milk, 1 tablespoon at a time, to get a pourable consistency. Spread over rolls. Makes 3 dozen.

The Battle Monument is located on Trophy Point at the U.S. Military Academy, West Point, New York. Dedicated to the men and officers of the Regular Army killed in the Civil War, the memorial shows "Fame" at the top of the column as a tribute to brave men. *Drawing by James Boujikan, courtesy of USMA, West Point.*

Cakes and Cookies

Apple Pound Cake

Jane Blankenship, Fort Lewis, Washington

> 1 cup butter or margarine, softened
> ½ cup vegetable shortening
> 2 cups granulated sugar
> 6 eggs
> 3 cups all-purpose flour
> ½ teaspoon baking powder
> ½ teaspoon salt
> 1½ teaspoons apple pie spice
> 1 cup apple cider or apple juice
> 1 teaspoon vanilla extract

Cream butter or margarine and shortening in large bowl. Gradually add sugar, beating until light and fluffy. Add eggs, one at a time, beating after each addition.

In another bowl, combine the next 4 ingredients. Add flour mixture to the creamed mixture alternately with the apple cider or juice, beginning and ending with flour mixture. Stir in vanilla.

Pour batter into a greased and floured 9-inch tube pan. Bake in a preheated oven at 325°F for 60–70 minutes or until a toothpick inserted in the center comes out clean. Serves 16.

Chewy Oatmeal Coconut Cookies

Stacy A. Hall, Berlin, West Germany

1¾ cups brown sugar
1¾ cups granulated sugar
2 cups oatmeal
5 cups all-purpose flour
2 teaspoons baking soda
2 teaspoons baking powder
1 teaspoon salt
4 eggs, beaten
2 teaspoons vanilla extract
1 pound butter or margarine, melted
2 cups shredded coconut

Combine the first 7 ingredients in a large bowl. Make a well in the center of the bowl and pour in eggs, vanilla, and melted butter. Stir with a wooden spoon or by hand until well blended. Add coconut and mix again.

Roll dough into walnut-size balls and place on greased cookie sheet. Flatten with fork.

Bake in a preheated oven at 350°F for 10 minutes, or until lightly browned. May be frozen after baking. Makes about 100 cookies.

Chinese Almond Cookies
Dorothy V. Egerland, Patrick AFB, Florida

1 cup butter or margarine
½ cup granulated sugar
2½ cups all-purpose flour, sifted
½ cup ground almonds
½ cup confectioner's sugar
1 teaspoon vanilla extract

In a large bowl, cream butter or margarine and granulated sugar. Add flour and almonds and mix well.

Knead lightly so that mixture will stick together. Add 1 teaspoon water if mixture is too dry. Shape into small balls about the size of a half dollar.

Place on greased cookie sheet about ¾ inch apart. Bake in a preheated oven at 350°F for 12–15 minutes or until they are firm to the touch.

Combine confectioner's sugar and vanilla in a small bowl. When cookies have cooled enough to handle, roll them in the sugar mixture. Makes about 3 dozen.

Chocolate Chip Date Nut Cake
Carol Diliberti, Fuerth, West Germany

This German recipe is delicious with hickory nuts.

> ½ *cup chopped dates*
> 1¾ *teaspoon baking soda, divided*
> 1½ *cups boiling water*
> ½ *cup shortening*
> 2 *eggs, beaten*
> 1½ *cups granulated sugar, divided*
> 1¼ *cups plus 3 tablespoons all-purpose flour*
> ¼ *teaspoon baking powder*
> ¼ *teaspoon salt*
> 1 *6-ounce package chocolate chips*
> ½ *cup chopped nuts*

Combine dates, 1 teaspoon baking soda, and boiling water in small bowl. Cool.

In a large bowl, cream shortening with eggs and 1 cup sugar. Add cooled date mixture and stir well.

Sift flour, baking powder, salt, and remaining ¾ teaspoon baking soda into the date mixture. Combine well. Pour into a greased and floured 9 x 13-inch pan.

Combine chocolate chips, nuts, and remaining ½ cup sugar. Sprinkle over batter. Bake in a preheated oven at 350°F for 35 minutes or until a toothpick inserted in the center comes out clean. Serves 15.

Creamy Caramel Layer Cake

Robbie Ann H. Cobb, Grand Forks, North Dakota

¾ cup butter or margarine
2 cups granulated sugar
3 cups all-purpose flour
2 teaspoons baking powder
1 cup milk
1 teaspoon vanilla extract
5 egg whites, at room temperature

Creamy Caramel Frosting
3 cups granulated sugar
2 cups whipping cream
¼ cup light corn syrup
1 teaspoon vanilla extract

In a large bowl, cream butter or margarine with sugar.

Sift flour and baking powder together in another bowl. Alternately add milk and flour to creamed mixture, beginning and ending with flour. Stir in vanilla. Mix well.

In a small bowl, beat egg whites until stiff peaks form. Fold into creamed mixture.

Turn into 2 9-inch round, greased, and floured pans. Bake in a preheated oven at 350°F for 25–30 minutes or until a wooden toothpick inserted in the center comes out clean.

While cake is baking, make frosting. Combine all ingredients except vanilla in a buttered, heavy saucepan. Cook over medium heat, stirring often, until a candy thermometer registers at the soft ball stage. Remove from heat and let cool slightly. Add vanilla. Beat until icing becomes spreadable.

When cake is done, let cool 10 minutes in pans. Turn out onto cake rack and let cool completely. Ice with Creamy Caramel Frosting. Serves 14.

Creme de Menthe Chocolate Cake
Joni Anger, USMA, West Point, New York

1 cup butter or margarine
6 tablespoons cocoa
1 cup water
2 cups all-purpose flour
2 cups granulated sugar
1 teaspoon baking soda
½ teaspoon salt
½ cup sour cream
2 eggs

Mint Frosting
2 cups powdered sugar
3 tablespoons creme de menthe
   liqueur
½ cup butter or margarine, softened

Glaze
6 ounces semisweet chocolate chips
6 tablespoons butter or margarine

Melt the butter or margarine with cocoa and water in a small saucepan.

In a large bowl, sift flour, sugar, baking soda, and salt.

In a small bowl, combine the sour cream and eggs.

Combine wet ingredients with dry by alternately adding cocoa mixture and sour cream mixture to the flour. Blend well.

Pour into a 9 x 13-inch greased and floured pan. Bake in a preheated oven at 350°F for 20–30 minutes or until a toothpick inserted in the center comes out clean. Cool in pan.

When cake is cool, make Mint Frosting. Combine all ingredients and spread over cooled cake.

To make Glaze, melt chocolate chips and butter. Mix well. Spread evenly over the Mint Frosting. Serves 24.

Donna's Applesauce Cake
Donna M. Hargraves, Powell, Wyoming

3 cups chunky applesauce
½ cup water
¾ cup vegetable oil
2 large eggs
3 cups all-purpose flour
2½ cups granulated sugar
1½ teaspoons baking soda
½ teaspoon salt
¼ teaspoon baking powder
2 tablespoons cinnamon
½ teaspoon ground allspice
½ teaspoon ground pumpkin pie spice
½ cup raisins

Frosting
1 8-ounce package cream cheese, softened
1 stick butter or margarine, softened
2 tablespoons vanilla extract
1 1-pound box confectioner's sugar
(approximately)

In a large bowl, combine applesauce, water, oil, and eggs. Mix well. Add remaining ingredients, stirring well after each addition.

Pour batter into a greased 9 x 12-inch pan. Bake in a preheated oven at 350°F for 45 minutes or until a toothpick inserted in the center comes out clean.

Cool cake in pan on wire rack. While cooling, make frosting. Cream together cream cheese, butter or margarine, and vanilla with enough confectioner's sugar to make spreadable frosting. Frost cake in pan when completely cool. Serves 15.

Filled Cupcakes
Naomi J. Moore, Altus AFB, Oklahoma

1 18¼-ounce package chocolate cake mix
½ cup Crisco
½ cup granulated sugar
½ 3½-ounce package vanilla pudding (not instant)
½ cup milk
1 teaspoon coconut flavoring

Prepare cupcakes according to package directions. Let cool 15 minutes.

While cupcakes are baking, beat Crisco and sugar together at high speed for 10 minutes.

In a medium saucepan, cook pudding and milk over medium heat until pudding thickens. Add to the Crisco mixture. Add coconut flavoring and mix well.

Fill a decorator bag with pudding filling. Squirt about 2 tablespoons into the center of each cupcake. Frost with your favorite frosting. Makes 2 dozen.

French Apple "Pie"

Sandy Duke, Eilson AFB, Alaska

1 1-pound, 4-ounce can apple pie filling
¾ cup granulated sugar
1 cup Bisquick, divided
1 egg
½ cup milk
3½ tablespoons butter or margarine, divided
⅓ cup brown sugar, firmly packed

Place apple pie filling in bottom of a 9 x 13-inch baking dish. Set aside.

In a small bowl, combine the granulated sugar, ½ cup Bisquick, egg, milk, and 2 teaspoons butter or margarine. Mix well. Pour over apple filling.

In a small bowl, combine remaining Bisquick, butter or margarine, and brown sugar. Crumble this mixture over top.

Bake in a preheated oven at 325°F for 55–60 minutes or until a toothpick inserted in the center comes out clean. Top should be golden brown. Serve warm with ice cream. Serves 8.

Fruit Cocktail Torte

Myra Hunt Rackley, Dallas, Georgia

Serve this torte with whipped cream for an added taste treat.

> 1¼ cups all-purpose flour, sifted
> 1 cup granulated sugar
> 1 teaspoon baking soda
> 1 teaspoon salt
> 1 egg, beaten
> 1 16-ounce can fruit cocktail
> ½ teaspoon vanilla extract
> 1 cup light brown sugar, lightly packed
> 1 cup chopped pecans

Mix flour, sugar, soda, and salt in a large bowl. Add the egg, fruit cocktail, and vanilla. Combine well.

Pour into a well-greased 9 x 13-inch pan. Sprinkle the brown sugar and nuts on top.

Bake in a preheated oven at 325°F for 45 minutes or until a toothpick inserted into the center comes out clean. Serves 8.

Gram's Banana Cake

Mrs. Joseph Kowal, Norwich, Connecticut

Especially good with cream cheese frosting!

  2 *cups all-purpose flour*
1½ *cups granulated sugar*
  1 *teaspoon baking soda*
  1 *teaspoon baking powder*
  ¼ *teaspoon salt*
  ½ *cup butter or margarine, softened*
  1 *cup milk*
  2 *tablespoons lemon juice*
  1 *cup mashed bananas (about 3 or 4 medium bananas)*
  2 *eggs*
  1 *teaspoon vanilla extract*
  ½ *cup chopped walnuts*

Combine dry ingredients in a large bowl. Add butter or margarine, milk mixed with lemon juice, and mashed bananas. Mix well after each addition.

Add eggs and vanilla. Stir well. Fold in nuts.

Pour into a greased 9 x 13-inch pan. Bake in a preheated oven at 350°F for 40–50 minutes or until a toothpick inserted in the center comes out clean.

Cool 10 minutes in pan, then remove from pan and cool completely. Frost if desired. Serves 18.

$100 Chocolate Cake

Ursula M. Phares, Millington, Tennessee

½ cup butter or margarine
2 cups granulated sugar
2 squares unsweetened chocolate, melted
2 eggs, beaten
1½ cups milk
2 cups cake flour
1 teaspoon salt
3 teaspoons baking powder
2 teaspoons vanilla extract
1 cup chopped walnuts

Icing
½ cup butter or margarine
1 square unsweetened chocolate
2½ cups confectioner's sugar
1 egg, beaten
1 teaspoon vanilla extract
1 teaspoon lemon juice
½ teaspoon salt
1 cup chopped walnuts

Cream butter or margarine with sugar in a small bowl. Add melted chocolate and eggs. Add milk.

Sift dry ingredients in a large bowl. Add walnuts and mix well. Combine wet and dry ingredients.

Turn mixture into 2 greased 9-inch round cake pans. Bake in a preheated oven at 350°F for 45 minutes or until a toothpick inserted into the cake comes out clean.

To make icing, melt butter or margarine with chocolate in the top of a double boiler.

In a medium bowl, combine the sugar, egg, lemon juice, and salt. Add the chocolate mixture and stir well. Add the walnuts and stir again. When cake has cooled completely, remove from pan and frost. Serves 8.

Pineapple Pound Cake

Mrs. Diana Dalla Betta, Camp Lejeune MCBC, North Carolina

1 cup butter, softened
½ cup margarine, softened
2½ cups granulated sugar
6 eggs
3 cups all-purpose flour
1 teaspoon baking powder
¼ cup evaporated milk
1 teaspoon vanilla extract
1 10½-ounce can crushed pineapple, drained

In a large bowl, cream butter and margarine with sugar until light and fluffy. Add eggs, beating well after each addition.

Mix in remaining ingredients and stir well. Pour batter into a greased and floured 9-inch Bundt pan.

Bake in a preheated oven at 300°F for 1½ hours or until a toothpick inserted in the center comes out clean. Cool 10 minutes in pan and then invert onto a serving dish. Serves 8.

Saucy Apple Swirl
Marie D. Hendrickson, Oneco, Florida

1 *cup brown sugar, lightly packed*
2 *tablespoons cinnamon*
1 *18.25-ounce box yellow cake mix*
3 *eggs, beaten*
1 *16-ounce jar applesauce*
1 *cup chopped pecans or walnuts*

Blend sugar and cinnamon together in a small bowl.

In a large bowl, combine cake mix with eggs and applesauce, using an electric mixer. Beat until all cake mix lumps are gone.

Pour half the batter into a greased 9½-inch tube pan. Sprinkle the cinnamon mixture and nuts evenly over the batter. Add remaining batter on top.

Bake in a preheated oven at 350°F for 35–45 minutes or until a toothpick inserted in center comes out clean. Cool in pan for 10 minutes. Invert onto plate. Serves 8.

Swedish Pineapple Nut Cake
Tina M. Corley, Bamberg, West Germany

2 *cups all-purpose flour*
2 *cups granulated sugar*
2 *teaspoons baking soda*
   pinch of salt
2 *eggs*
1 *20-ounce can crushed pineapple with juice*
1 *teaspoon vanilla extract*
1 *cup chopped walnuts*

Frosting
1 *8-ounce package cream cheese, softened*
½ *cup butter or margarine, softened*
1 *teaspoon vanilla extract*
2 *cups confectioner's sugar*
½ *cup chopped walnuts*

Combine dry ingredients in a large bowl. Using an electric mixer, add eggs, pineapple, and vanilla. Fold in nuts.

Pour into a greased 15½ x 10 x 1-inch pan. Bake in a preheated oven at 350°F for 20–25 minutes or until a toothpick inserted in the center comes out clean. Cool and frost in the pan.

To make frosting, mix all ingredients together in a small bowl. Blend well. Refrigerate cake before serving. Serves 15.

Unbelievable Peanut Butter Cookies

Lonnie Jo Peterson, Holloman AFB, New Mexico

1 cup granulated sugar
1 teaspoon vanilla extract
1 egg
1 cup peanut butter, smooth or chunky

Combine sugar, vanilla, and egg in a medium bowl. Mix well. Add peanut butter and stir until well blended.

Drop by teaspoonfuls onto an ungreased cookie sheet. Bake in a preheated oven at 350°F for 15 minutes or until cookies are set. Makes 3 dozen.

White Fruit Cake

Mrs. Morris H. Faber, Jr., MDW Cameron Station, Alexandria, Virginia

1½ pounds candied pineapple
1½ pounds red and green cherries
1 12-ounce box golden raisins
1 6-ounce package flaked coconut
1 pound pecans
1 pound almonds
6 cups all-purpose flour, divided
1 pound butter or margarine
2 cups granulated sugar
9 eggs
½ cup fresh orange juice
½ light corn syrup
½ cup Apple Jack brandy
1 teaspoon vanilla extract
additional brandy for soaking

Chop fruit and nuts. Combine with 2 cups of flour in a medium bowl. Stir well to coat. Set aside.

In a large bowl, cream butter or margarine and sugar until light and fluffy. Add eggs, one at a time, beating well after each addition.

In a small bowl, combine juice, corn syrup, ½ cup brandy, and vanilla. Alternately add liquid and flour to creamed mixture. Mix well after each addition. Fold in fruit and nuts. Stir well.

Grease 2 tube pans and line with brown paper. Divide batter between pans and bake in a preheated oven at 250°F for 2 hours, 45 minutes, or until toothpick inserted in the center comes out clean. Avoid overcooking.

Cool cakes thoroughly in pans and then turn out. Wrap each in a brandy-soaked cloth. Do not pour brandy directly on cakes. Place in an airtight container.

Check after 1 week. Soak cloths again in brandy and rewrap. Store 1 month to 6 weeks before serving. May be frozen after aging. Serves 40.

Desserts

Angel Pie

Kim Guariglia, Darmstadt, West Germany

> 4 *eggs, separated*
> 1 *teaspoon cream of tartar*
> 1½ *cups granulated sugar, divided*
> 1½ *lemons, juice and pulp*
> ½ *lemon rind, grated*
> ½ *pint heavy cream, whipped*

Beat the egg whites with an electric mixer on high in a medium bowl until foamy. Add cream of tartar. Beat until stiff. Slowly add 1 cup sugar, beating constantly.

Spread this mixture into a well-greased 9-inch pie pan. Bake in a preheated 300°F oven for 45 minutes or until top begins to brown.

Let stand until completely cool. While cooling, make filling. Cook egg yolks, lemon juice, pulp, and rind, and remaining ½ cup sugar in a double boiler over high heat. Stir constantly until thickened. Cool completely.

Flatten the crust slightly with a fork and spread lemon filling over the top. Cover with whipped cream. Refrigerate 24 hours before serving. Serves 6.

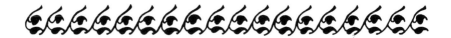

Applesauce Cheese Bars
Kathy Penrose, Sun City, California

2½ cups uncooked rolled oats
1 cup unsweetened apple butter
1½ cups unsweetened applesauce
1 teaspoon cinnamon
½ cup honey
1½ cups grated cheddar cheese, divided
½ cup chopped walnuts or pecans

Mix oats, apple butter, applesauce, cinnamon honey, and 1 cup of the cheese in a large bowl. Stir well.

Spread mixture evenly in a greased 9 x 13-inch pan.

Combine remaining cheese and the nuts in a small bowl. Spread over top of oats mixture.

Bake in a preheated oven at 350°F for 25 minutes or until top is lightly browned. Cool to room temperature, then refrigerate for at least 2 hours before serving. Cut into squares. Serves 12.

Blanche's Drunken Bread Puddin'
Blanche Hann, Camarillo, California

This has been modified from an old English recipe by adding the Bourbon Sauce.

> 1 12-ounce loaf French bread, torn into bite-size pieces
> 1 quart milk
> 3 eggs, lightly beaten
> 1½ cups granulated sugar
> 2 tablespoons vanilla extract

Bourbon Sauce
> ½ stick butter or margarine
> ½ cup granulated sugar
> 1 egg, lightly beaten
> 1 tablespoon bourbon whiskey

In a large bowl, soak the bread in the milk until mushy, about 20 minutes.

In a small bowl, combine eggs, sugar, and vanilla. Mix and add to the bread. Stir thoroughly. Turn into a lightly greased 2-quart casserole dish. Set aside.

Make the Bourbon Sauce by heating the butter or margarine with sugar until dissolved. Remove from heat and add egg. Beat by hand until foamy. Add whiskey. Pour over pudding.

Bake, uncovered, in a preheated oven at 350°F for 1 hour or until set. Serves 12.

Buster Bar Dessert

Kathleen Marshall, Fort Sam Houston, Texas

42 *fudge sandwich cookies*
¼ *cup butter or margarine, melted*
½ *gallon vanilla ice cream, softened*
1 *14-ounce jar chocolate fudge topping*
1 *cup coarsely chopped Spanish peanuts*
1 *8-ounce container Cool Whip*

Crush cookies in a blender or food processor. Mix with butter or margarine.

Reserving one-third of the cookie crumbs, press the remainder into a 9 x 13-inch pan. Cover and place in freezer for 1 hour.

Spread softened ice cream on top of cookie crumbs. Cover and freeze until solid, about 2 hours.

Top with chocolate fudge, peanuts, and Cool Whip in that order. Place reserved crumbs on top. Cover and freeze for 1 hour. Serve straight from freezer. Serves 12.

Butter Nut Chews

Barbara A. Ward, Killeen, Texas

    2 eggs
    2 cups light or dark brown sugar, firmly packed
    1 teaspoon vanilla extract
    ½ cup butter or margarine, melted
 1½ cups all-purpose flour
    2 teaspoons baking powder
    ½ teaspoon salt
    1 cup chopped nuts
    1 cup raisins
    1 cup grated coconut

Whip eggs in a large bowl until light and foamy. Beat in sugar, vanilla, and butter or margarine until creamy.

In a separate bowl, combine flour, baking powder, and salt. Add to egg-sugar mixture. Stir in nuts, raisins, and coconut.

Spread evenly in a greased 9 x 13 x 2-inch pan. Bake in a preheated oven at 350°F for 25–30 minutes or until a wooden toothpick inserted in the center comes out clean.

Cool 10–15 minutes. Cut into bars. Makes 2 dozen.

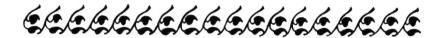

Cary's Favorite Cheesecake
Louisa Otis, USCG LORAN "C" Station, Sylt, West Germany

Crust
1¼ cups graham cracker crumbs
¼ cup butter or margarine, melted
½ teaspoon cinnamon

Filling
3 8-ounce packages cream cheese, softened
3 eggs, separated
1 1-ounce square unsweetened chocolate, melted
1 teaspoon vanilla extract
½ teaspoon rum extract
½ cup rum or brandy
1 cup granulated sugar

Topping
2 cups sour cream
2 tablespoons granulated sugar
1 teaspoon vanilla extract

In a small bowl, combine graham cracker crumbs, melted butter or margarine, and cinnamon. Press into the bottom and up the sides of a 9-inch springform pan. Bake in a preheated oven at 350°F for 10 minutes.

In a large bowl, beat together with electric mixer at high speed the cream cheese, egg yolks, melted chocolate, vanilla and rum extracts, and rum or brandy until smooth and creamy.

In a separate bowl, beat egg whites until stiff peaks form, then continue to beat while gradually adding sugar. Fold into cream cheese mixture.

Pour into baked crust and bake in a preheated oven at 350°F for 30 minutes. Turn off heat and leave cheesecake in oven until cool.

Combine topping ingredients. Pour over top of cheesecake when cake is cool. Bake in a preheated oven at 400°F for 5 minutes. Remove from oven immediately and cool to room temperature. Refrigerate at least 2 hours before serving. Serves 12.

Cherry Bars

Debra E. Beach, St. Robert, Missouri

1½ cups all-purpose flour
1 teaspoon salt
½ teaspoon baking soda
¾ cup uncooked rolled oats
½ cup butter or margarine
1 cup brown sugar, firmly packed
2 21-ounce cans cherry pie filling

Sift together flour, salt, and baking soda in a small bowl. Add oats.

In a large bowl, cream butter or margarine and sugar until light and fluffy.

Add the flour mixture to the creamed mixture. Stir until crumbly. Pat half of this mixture into the bottom of a greased 7½ x 11¾-inch pan.

Pour cherry pie filling over oats. Sprinkle remaining oats mixture on top.

Bake in a preheated oven at 350°F for 30 minutes or until top is lightly browned. Cool completely and cut into squares. Serves 8.

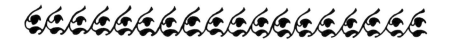

Chocolate Mousse
Judi Burnett, El Paso, Texas

For mocha mousse, use coffee instead of water.

    1 *6-ounce package semisweet chocolate bits*
    5 *tablespoons boiling water or hot coffee*
    4 *eggs, separated*
    2 *tablespoons golden rum or 1 tablespoon vanilla*
        whipped cream for garnish

Melt chips with water or coffee in the top of a double boiler.
In a small glass bowl, beat egg whites until stiff.
In a large bowl, beat egg yolks. Add rum or vanilla to yolk mixture. Add chocolate mixture to yolks. Gently fold egg whites into chocolate mixture.
Refrigerate two hours. Serve with a dollop of whipped cream. Serves 5.

Cream Cheese Fudge
Karen J. Brownfield, NAS Lemoore, California

    4 *cups powdered sugar, sifted*
    1 *8-ounce package cream cheese, softened*
    4 *1-ounce squares unsweetened chocolate, melted*
    1 *teaspoon vanilla extract*
        dash salt
  ½ *cup chopped nuts*

In a large mixing bowl, gradually add sugar to cream cheese, using an electric mixer. Beat until well blended.
Stir in remaining ingredients, except nuts, and mix well. Fold in nuts.
Spread into a greased 8-inch-square pan and chill overnight. Cut into 1½-inch squares. Makes 25 squares.

Dad's Favorite Pecan Chews

Betty Compton Simmons, Lindsey Air Station, West Germany

¾ cup all-purpose flour
1 tablespoon instant coffee
½ teaspoon salt
2 eggs
1 cup granulated sugar
½ cup butter or margarine, melted
1 teaspoon vanilla extract
½ cup chopped pecans

Icing
1 cup confectioner's sugar
½ teaspoon vanilla extract
1–2 tablespoons milk

Sift together flour, instant coffee, and salt in a small bowl. Set aside.

In a medium bowl, beat eggs until foamy. Gradually add sugar and continue beating till thick and creamy. Stir in melted butter or margarine and vanilla.

Add dry ingredients and stir until well blended. Stir in nuts.

Pour into a greased, 8-inch-square pan. Bake in a preheated oven at 350°F for 30–35 minutes or until a toothpick inserted in the center comes out clean.

While chews are cooling, make icing. Combine confectioner's sugar and vanilla in a small bowl. Gradually add enough milk to get a creamy consistency.

When completely cool, drizzle with icing and cut into squares. Serves 12.

Frozen Peanut Butter Pie
Senior Chief Randall R. Weir, NTC San Diego, California

Crust
2⅓ cups graham cracker crumbs
¾ cup butter or margarine
⅓ cup superfine granulated sugar
⅔ cup sifted cocoa powder

Filling
2¾ pints vanilla ice cream,
    softened
½ cup peanut butter
2 ounces semisweet chocolate
    bits

Topping
½ cup granulated sugar
⅓ cup water
1 tablespoon corn syrup
2¼ ounces sweet chocolate, melted
¼ cup whipping cream

1 cup prepared whipped topping
    (approximately)

To make crust, combine ingredients until well blended. Press firmly into the bottom of a 9-inch pie plate. Freeze for about 2 hours.

In a large bowl, combine ice cream, peanut butter, and semisweet chocolate. Stir by hand or with an electric mixer on low. Do not over-whip. Spoon into prepared crust. Freeze immediately until solid, at least 2 hours.

When ready to serve, make topping. Combine sugar, water, corn syrup, and chocolate in saucepan. Bring to boil. Immediately remove from heat and stir until smooth.

In separate pan, heat cream until just before the boiling point. Stir into chocolate mixture until smooth. Pour over frozen ice cream pie. Top with prepared whipped topping. Serves 8.

Frozen Strawberry Dessert

Mrs. Bruno Kolodgie, Nanticoke, Pennsylvania

1 8-ounce package cream cheese, softened
¾ cup granulated sugar
2 bananas, sliced
1 10-ounce package frozen sliced strawberries, partially thawed
1 20-ounce can crushed pineapple, well drained
½ cup chopped walnuts
1 8-ounce container Cool Whip, thawed

Mix cream cheese and sugar in large bowl. Add bananas, strawberries, pineapple, and nuts. Combine well.

Fold in Cool Whip and turn into a 4 x 10-inch pan. Cover and freeze at least 24 hours. Take out 15 minutes before serving. Slice into 2-inch slices. Serves 8.

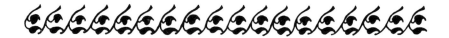

Georgia Street Slices

Jeannie R. O'Neill, North Reading, Massachusetts

1 *cup butter or margarine, divided*
¼ *cup granulated sugar*
5 *tablespoons cocoa*
2 *cups graham cracker crumbs*
1 *cup shredded coconut*
1 *egg, beaten*
2 *cups confectioner's sugar*
2 *tablespoons instant dry vanilla pudding mix*
¼ *scant cup milk*
3 *squares semisweet chocolate*
2 *tablespoons butter or margarine*

In a double boiler, melt ½ cup butter or margarine with the granulated sugar and cocoa.

When melted, remove from heat and stir in graham cracker crumbs, coconut, and egg. Spread this mixture into the bottom of a 9-inch-square pan. Refrigerate for 1 hour.

Mix together confectioner's sugar, vanilla pudding mix, and ½ cup butter. Add milk gradually so that mixture is stiff enough to spread on the graham cracker mixture.

Spread sugar mixture over the chilled crumbs. Return to refrigerator for 1 hour.

In a double boiler, melt the chocolate squares with the 2 tablespoons butter or margarine. Spread chocolate layer on top of chilled sugar layer. Cut into squares and refrigerate for at least 1 hour. Must be kept refrigerated until served. Makes about 4 dozen.

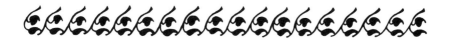

Lady Finger Delight
Sylvia P. Radom, Miami, Florida

6 *eggs, separated*
2 *lemons, juiced*
 rind of 1 lemon
1½ *cups granulated sugar, divided*
1 *3-ounce package lemon gelatin*
1 *cup boiling water*
2 *packages lady fingers, 16 fingers each, split in half lengthwise*
½ *pint whipping cream*
1 *cup shredded coconut*

Combine egg yolks with lemon juice and grated rind of 1 lemon in the top of a double boiler. Mix well.

Add ¾ cup of sugar and cook until thick, stirring constantly. Cool.

Dissolve gelatin in boiling water. Let cool until tepid, about 15 minutes. Add to egg yolk–lemon mixture.

Beat egg whites with remaining sugar in a small bowl until they form stiff peaks. Fold into egg yolk–gelatin mixture.

Line the sides and bottom of an 8-inch springform pan with lady fingers. Pour in lemon mixture, cover and refrigerate overnight.

The next day, whip the cream in a small bowl. Cover top of cake. Sprinkle generously with shredded coconut. Serves 8.

Macadamia Nut Pie

Mrs. Monique E. Jones, Malmstrom AFB, Great Falls, Montana

3 *eggs*
1 *cup light corn syrup*
⅔ *cup granulated sugar*
7 *ounces salted macadamia nuts, coarsely chopped*
2 *tablespoons butter, melted*
1 *teaspoon vanilla extract*
1 *unbaked pie shell*
2 *cups whipped cream (optional)*

Beat eggs, corn syrup, and sugar in a medium bowl until well blended.

Stir in nuts, butter, and vanilla. Mix well. Pour into pie shell.

Bake in a preheated oven at 350°F for 50 minutes or until filling is set. Cool about 1 hour and then refrigerate up to 3 days. Top with whipped cream, if desired, just before serving. Serves 6.

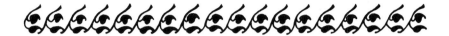

Mile Hi Strawberry Pie

Marie Marchesini, Hanscom AFB, Massachusetts

1 10-ounce package frozen strawberries, thawed
¾ cup granulated sugar
2 egg whites
1 tablespoon lemon juice
¼ teaspoon salt
⅛ teaspoon vanilla extract
2 cups Cool Whip
1 9- or 10-inch pie shell, baked

Place thawed strawberries, sugar, egg whites, lemon juice, and salt in large mixing bowl.

With electric mixer, beat on medium speed for 15 minutes or until mixture forms stiff peaks.

Stir vanilla into Cool Whip and fold carefully into strawberry mixture. Pile lightly into pie shell. Freeze, uncovered, overnight. Serve directly from freezer. Serves 6.

Mini Cheesecakes

Mrs. Susan J. Runkle, Kaneohe Bay MCAS, Hawaii

> 2 *8-ounce packages cream cheese, softened*
> 2 *eggs*
> 1 *cup granulated sugar*
> ½ *teaspoon vanilla extract*
> 24 *vanilla wafer cookies*
> 1 *21-ounce can cherry or blueberry pie filling*

In a large mixing bowl, combine cream cheese, eggs, sugar, and vanilla. Beat with an electric mixer until mixture is smooth and creamy.

On a cookie sheet, place 2 dozen small foil baking cups. Place 1 wafer, flat side down, in each cup.

Place about 1 tablespoon of cheese mixture on top of each wafer. Bake in a preheated oven at 350°F for 15 minutes or until mixture is set.

Remove from oven and cool completely. Top with cherry or blueberry pie filling. Serves 6.

No-Crust Coconut Pie

Shelly Tebo, NAS Norfolk, Virginia

2 cups milk
¾ cup granulated sugar
½ cup Bisquick
4 eggs
¼ cup butter or margarine, melted
1½ teaspoons vanilla extract
1 cup shredded coconut

In a large bowl, combine all ingredients except coconut, using an electric mixer on low speed. Mix for 3 minutes.

Pour mixture evenly into 2 9-inch ungreased pie plates. Let stand 5 minutes. Divide the coconut equally on top of each pie.

Bake in a preheated 350°F oven for 40 minutes or until mixture is set and coconut lightly browned. Serves 12.

Texas Whiskey Balls

Peggy Marshall, Amelia Island, Florida

1 12-ounce package vanilla wafers
1 cup light brown sugar, firmly packed
2 teaspoons cocoa
1 cup finely chopped pecans
½ cup whiskey, brandy, or rum
2 tablespoons light corn syrup
1½ cups confectioner's sugar
(approximately)

Crush wafers into crumbs. In a large bowl, combine crumbs, brown sugar, cocoa, and pecans. Mix well.

Add whiskey, brandy, or rum, and corn syrup. Mix well.

Shape mixture into 1-inch-diameter balls. Roll in confectioner's sugar. Pack in additional confectioner's sugar in a covered container. Will keep up to 6 weeks. Makes about 3 dozen.

Walnut Peach Torte

Colette Landsteiner, US Naval Station, Rota, Spain

Crust
1 *cup butter or margarine, softened*
2 *cups all-purpose flour*
1 *teaspoon salt*
1 *egg*

Filling
3 *eggs, separated*
2 *cups granulated sugar, divided*
2 *teaspoons lemon juice*
4 *cups sliced peaches, divided*
3 *tablespoons tapioca*
¼ *teaspoon cream of tartar*
¼ *cup chopped walnuts (approximately)*

Blend together all crust ingredients except egg in a small bowl. Add egg and stir well. Pat into the bottom of a 9 x 13-inch baking dish. Bake, uncovered, in a preheated oven at 425°F for 15 minutes or until browned.

In a saucepan, combine egg yolks, 1¼ cups sugar, lemon juice, 3 cups of peaches, and tapioca. Cook on medium heat until mixture comes to a full boil. Boil 1 minute, cool slightly (about 10–15 minutes), and add remaining peaches. Pour on top of crust.

Using an electric mixer, beat egg whites with cream of tartar in a small bowl. Slowly add remaining ¾ cup sugar and beat until stiff. Fold in walnuts and pour over peaches.

Bake, uncovered, in a preheated oven at 350°F for 15–20 minutes or until egg whites have turned light brown. Serves 12.

Index